A Bigger Boat

Mary Burritt
Christiansen
Poetry Series

Mary Burritt Christiansen Poetry Series
V. B. Price, Series Editor

Also available in the University of New Mexico Press
Mary Burritt Christiansen Poetry Series:

A Bigger Boat

The Unlikely Success of the

Albuquerque Poetry Slam Scene

EDITED BY

Susan McAllister,

Don McIver,

Mikaela Renz,

and Daniel S. Solis

UNIVERSITY OF NEW MEXICO PRESS

ALBUQUERQUE

13 12 11 10 09 08   1 2 3 4 5 6

Library of Congress Cataloging-in-Publication Data

A bigger boat : the unlikely success of the Albuquerque poetry slam scene /
edited by Susan McAllister ... [et al.].
       p. cm.
ISBN 978-0-8263-4483-0 (pbk. : alk. paper)
1. American poetry—20th century. 2. American poetry—21st century.
3. Poetry slams—New Mexico—Albuquerque—History—20th century.
4. Poetry slams—New Mexico—Albuquerque—History—21st century.
5. Oral interpretation of poetry—Competitions. 6. Poetry—Authorship.
I. McAllister, Susan.
       PS615.B495 2008
       811'.608—dc22
                 2008002810

Grateful acknowledgment is given to the following publications in which
several of the poems in this anthology have been previously published.
Adam Rubinstein's "Courting the Spark" from *Meet me an hour ago* by
Destructible Heart Press. Damien Flores's "Una Novena pa la Tierra" from
Novena of Mud by Destructible Heart Press. Laura E. J. Moran's "Misfits"
from *Live Bait* (2005). Carol Lewis's "War" originally appeared in *the rag*,
July 2006, and is reprinted here with permission.

t t t

Designed and typeset by Mina Yamashita.
Text composed in Utopia Std, a typeface designed
by Robert Slimbach for Adobe in 1989 and in
ITC Legacy Sans Std. designed in 1992 by Ronald Arnholm.
Display composed in Frutiger 77 Black Condensed,
designed by Adrian Frutiger in 1976.

Printed by Thomson-Shore, Inc. on 55# Natures Natural.

In the relay that is community building, we,

today, pick up where they, yesterday, left off.

This book is dedicated to Gene Frumkin (1928–2007),

Trinidad Sanchez (1943–2006), Ken Hunt (1970–2005),

and all those, here and gone, that came before.

Contents

Chapter Four: ABQ Poetry Brings NPS Home—the Organizers' Story / 125

Chapter Five: NPS 2005 and the ABQ Slam Team Champions' Story / 167

Chapter Six: ABQ Aftermath / 275

List of Illustrations

DANIEL S. SOLIS
Foreword

Fierce protector and gentle champion of Slam poetry in Albuquerque, Daniel S. Solis has eight city championships, three regional individual championships, a Taos Poetry Tag Team Championship, and international team and individual championships. He was a member of the National Poetry Slam Championship team from Boston 1992 and Asheville 1995.

Watching my community come together for the days and nights of the 2005 National Poetry Slam (NPS 2005) was one of the most exciting and gratifying experiences of my life. But it was not, could not ever be, more important than one poet onstage ascending to new levels of her craft and art, could not ever be more important than a rapt audience and the communication between the two—vital and ferocious, passionate and precise. This is for me the realization, the embodiment, of community—not the description, but the actuality, the living thing itself.

To begin to understand this relationship is to begin to understand how communities are built. There are no shortcuts, no easy formulas. The process is just plain hard work, and oftentimes frustrating, but the rewards are always worth more than the effort, whether that reward be organizing and taking part in the largest poetry event in the world or listening to one poet fold her wings and drop from a great metaphoric height, her words and emotions tearing a new space into the fabric of one's consciousness, conscience, leaving something at once bright and raw and breathless. In the end, it all comes down to that one poet, taking that walk up to the mic, that moment before she begins to speak, when she plummets into the space that separates us, closing that gap in the furious holy rush of the poem 'til the place is silent and the only thing that matters is her next word, her next phrase, moving us toward the space where we become one for an instant, in epiphany, in terror, in redemption, in laughter, in triumph, in understanding, THAT moment, when the poem is all that matters.

A poet stands furled at the mic, a gift coiled inside her glowing fist. In the midst of smoke, bar shuffle, and peripheral clatter, minds lean toward booze or nicotine or sex or any distraction to ease whatever boredom or pain or restlessness the audience grapples with this night. A beat, a sharp intake of breath, and her first words spill into the murk and sonic clutter of the room:

I don't know how to pray
never went to church
never had a sliver thin host melting on my tongue
I was never dipped back into the river
But I did find my own religion
Born out of a five-year-old's faith

Her voice, a small boat of light and music, parts the waves of predictable, mundane banter. The woman at the mic is a hawk diving toward the climax of her poem, splitting the sky of the barroom's attention 'til people cannot look away or speak or even lift their drinks:

By the time I arrived you were back in the hospital
your T-count low
and all I could think to say to you were
nervous chattering things

▼ ▼ ▼

for the first time in my life
I wished I had been born
with an old religion burned into my tongue
not this superstitious
untried
faith of one

The only sound now is the woman at the mic pleading with the gods to make this right:

that's when my five-year-old's words
came out of my mouth
please pretty please
I said out loud to the television set
c'mon baby c'mon baby c'mon baby
deep into your cells
please
I pleaded
I pleaded over your body
like you were a lottery ticket

I did it wrong
because if I knew how to pray
I would have done a better job
when I came to see you

when I begged for your life ▪

Figure 1. Traci Paris at the Dingo Bar.
Courtesy of Michael Hudock

As she hits the last line, the space between the poet and this Monday night bar crowd is gone. Each person knows that this moment is what brought them out tonight—whether they came to hear poetry or not—this moment of oneness, of deliverance from the daily dross.

The room erupts in a roar, drinks are drained, people look at each other in amazement, and Traci Paris leaves the stage. It is 1996, and the evening's host, Matthew John Conley, weaves his way back to the mic to guide the audience through another edition of Poetry and Beer at the Fabulous Dingo Bar on Gold Street in downtown Albuquerque. ▪

MARC SMITH
Preface

Creator of the Poetry Slam in Chicago in the 1980s, Marc Smith (Slampapi) is the longtime host of the Uptown Poetry Slam at the Green Mill and has been a performance poetry innovator.

In 2006 I traveled to Albuquerque to participate in a benefit for Gary Glazner's Alzheimer's Poetry Project. Gary Mex Glazner was the west coast force behind the 1990 Poetry Slam competition between San Francisco, New York, and Chicago. It was the seed that inspired the now-annual National Poetry Slams that have expanded to include nearly eighty competing cities, hundreds of poets, and thousands of enthusiastic audience members.

I was grateful to have the opportunity to return to Albuquerque. Over a decade ago I officiated, assisted, and performed at an early manifestation of the now well-established National Teen Slam. It was a fantastic event that ended with the kids throwing out the scoring system and performing their poems without judging because "the points were not the point"; the point was that they were expressing themselves with passion and poetry.

I was unable to attend the NPS 2005 staged in Albuquerque. I heard that other than an unseemly and ungrateful altercation on the final night, it was the most well-organized, well-attended, and joyous National Slam to date. That was quite a boast. There have been nineteen national slams, three of them in Chicago. Many were as sensational as a Broadway spectacular, and some pretty horrible flops. Frankly, I had become suspect of the bravado many slam poets and producers attached to their accomplishments.

I have known the Slam organizers of Albuquerque and the surrounding Southwest for quite some time and have great respect for their integrity, their no bullshit approach. It's similar to my own and the values that propel the Green Mill's Uptown Poetry Slam where it all began. But the slam and the spotlight can sometimes twist the hearts and minds of aspiring poets and organizers and change them from modest personalities into egocentric blah blah blahs grabbing for the bling bling bling. What would I find in Albuquerque?

I found the essence of why I and others have devoted our uncompensated time, energy, and material resources to this movement I started over twenty years ago. I found the spark and dazzle of hope, of purpose, of joy in the eyes and voices and hearts of the people who witnessed and participated in the event. The energy of those four days did not diminish on the final night. It gave birth, the latest birth in a line of births, and inspiration.

From the restaurant owners who catered to the crowds and served coffee and chile peppers to the spittin' spoutin' poets who seemed to never get enough to the cultural directors, programmers, and institutions that assisted the grassroots organizers; from the security forces wary of the ragtag tribe of slammers to the teachers and professors enlightened by the possibilities of what slam could do for the kids in their classrooms—it was all the same: poetry is a powerful, passionate art form that opens the doors of expression to all peoples and for all peoples, young old, rich poor, native or imported from beyond the beyond.

This anthology is a glimpse at the deep-rooted southwestern lineage of Slam, particularly Albuquerque's outstanding contribution to the national and international movement. Slam by intention is horizontal, a growing tree, an inverted pyramid. The collective actions of regional organizers, poets, and audience give it its strength. Each of us stands on each other's shoulders. Each of our voices joins the choir of voices seeking the truth of our common experience.

Proud? Sure I could say, and would say, that I'm proud of my association with the southwestern Slam community and proud of their achievements, honored that they asked me to write this preface introducing their proud collection of poetic works. But the true word is grateful—grateful that people are serving and helping people through Slam to find their voices, to experience the flesh and blood of performance, to learn about one another, and to shed the isolation and alienation prevalent in our high-tech, money-motivated, global-gobbling society; grateful that slammers, good and bad, are seekers perusing ideals that may just tip the human experience one feather more toward the awakened experience of truly and divinely being alive. ■

EDITORS
Introduction

In August 2005, Albuquerque's Poetry Slam team took top prize in the National Poetry Slam (NPS) Championships for the first time. This feat was all the more remarkable because Albuquerque hosted the event that year for the first time. That summer, for five nights and four days, downtown Albuquerque was transformed into a city of poetry, with five hundred performance poets arriving to vie for the titles of team and individual National Poetry Slam Champions. The efforts of its organizers and the quality of its performers allowed Albuquerque to host and win the largest poetry show on earth, despite its perpetual underdog complex.

Albuquerque's double success with NPS 2005, successes impossible to explain without recounting the history of Poetry Slam in Albuquerque, is a story of one step forward, two steps back, as setbacks followed hard on the heels of each small success. Over time, Albuquerque Slam has grown in faith and confidence. It took ten years for Albuquerque to reach its moment of glory—from the very first Albuquerque Slam team sent to Nationals in 1995 to the finals stage in 2005—ten years of tireless grassroots efforts to build the talent, passion, and competence needed to host—and win—NPS in Albuquerque. Just as there is no substitute for grassroots community building, there can be no meaningful discussion of NPS 2005 without recognizing the poets and poetry that built the 'Burque scene.

The book is organized roughly in chronological order. The history is told by multiple witnesses and participants, in some cases about events almost fifteen years ago. As is often the case, these historical accounts vary, even as each provides its own window of truth. Chapter 1 gives a sneak preview of team poems from the final stage at NPS 2005. Chapter 2 focuses on the growing presence of performance poetry and Slam poets in Albuquerque from 1990–1994. Chapter 3 represents the Slam years from 1995–2005, starting with the first year Albuquerque sent a Slam team to compete in the National Poetry Slam, with mixed results but garnering more national respect with each passing year. Chapter 4 tells the organizers' story from bidding for Albuquerque to host the Nationals through the craziness of four nonstop days of poets, poetry, competition, and overwhelming audience turnout, which Danny Solis foretold in his admonitions that we needed "a bigger boat" in order to survive. Chapter 5 gives a window into the event itself, from daytime events at the National Hispanic Cultural Center to the court intrigue of the finals stage, culminating in the individual poetry championship shared by Anis Mojgani of Portland and Janean Livingston of Ft. Worth and the team championship for Albuquerque. Chapter 6 takes a look at the Albuquerque poetry and art scene in the wake of the NPS storm. We're still riding that wave in our bigger and better boats.

This book celebrates the moments when barriers fall and we experience something singular, as part of a whole greater than the sum of the parts. The 2005 Albuquerque Team winning the NPS championship in its own hometown could be seen as a crowning achievement to NPS itself, hailed by many veteran and new slammers alike as the best NPS ever. Albuquerque hosting the biggest and best NPS in the fifteen-year history of the event and the 'Burque team winning in the same year makes a fitting crescendo to the first ten years of Poetry Slam in the city and leaves us with hope that the next ten years will be even more productive, more inclusive, with more passion lived and even bigger dreams cultivated and brought to fruition.

Ten years of poetry and organizing efforts built the 'Burque scene, and for five nights and four magical days in August 2005, moments piled up in the streets of downtown Albuquerque, new home to the greatest National Poetry Slam to date and to the first Albuquerque team to become National Slam Champions. ▪

Figure 2. Downtown Albuquerque Welcomes NPS 2005. *Courtesy of David Huang*

Chapter One

In Medias Res—NPS Finals 2005

The 2005 National Poetry Slam was nonstop poetry action, from 4:00 a.m. ciphers in hotel rooms and on balconies to kids' shows to roof-raising Slam competition performances by top-caliber national poets Roger Bonair Agard, Anis Mojgani, Rachel McKibbens, Christa Bell, and Corinna Bain, to name just a few.

Daytime events, workshops, and special readings at the National Hispanic Cultural Center (NHCC) celebrated poetry from the Latino, African-American, Gay/Lesbian/ TG/Bi, Asian, Native American, and Women's communities. Head-to-Head Haiku flowed from the basement theater of the Harwood Art Center. Local bookstores and community centers hosted readings and parties. Poets traveled to per- form at jails and senior centers, charter high schools and assisted living centers. These events reflected the grassroots presence of poets in the wider community—the hallmark and foundation of the Albuquerque poetry scene.

Slam competitions were held during the evening at venues throughout downtown. There were poets at the Launchpad, poets at the El Rey, poets at all the theatres at the National Hispanic Cultural Center, poets at the National Institute of Flamenco. Poets and audience spilled out of venues into the streets of downtown Albuquerque to the tune of over 22,000 poets and poetry lovers during the run of NPS 2005. The 2,300-seat venue at the Albuquerque Convention Center Kiva Auditorium was sold out for the Final Championship event. Tickets were actually being scalped just outside the building, going for fifty dollars a pop, a handsome profit for those doing the selling. Those lucky enough to buy a seat witnessed Albuquerque's hometown team winning the Championship—the first time a host city team had taken the event since 1992.

Although poetry is the main competition at NPS, there's a strong under-and-sometimes-over-the-top current of city rivalry. Not only are city teams competing against each other for the Championship title, but because the event itself rotates from city to city year to year, there is also a subtle sizing up of the organizers. Which Slam scene puts on the best show? Whose city brings the best audiences? Who does best at their own event?

Stakes were high in Albuquerque. Some of our poets have had strong national presence in the Slam scene for a long time, despite the fact that Albuquerque continued to have quite the reputation as a perpetual underdog. Organizers and the Albuquerque Slam Team were both under intense scrutiny with a lot to prove. There was much more at stake on the finals stage than just the NPS Team Championship title. The team from LA Green was going for a third win, and they were the subject of a documentary, with a film crew following them everywhere. Charlotte was absolutely positive they were going to win—uncannily positive, with blog posts prior to the event practically guaranteeing a win. One of Ft. Worth's team members, Janean Livingston, used five of her poems in the individual competition, ultimately tying with Anis Mojgani of Portland for the Individual Championship. Would she be able to help her team too?

By the finals stage, the best of the best are represented. The poems have been honed and perfected over months and sometimes years. The difference in competition often comes down to performance and the ability to capture the crowd. Regardless, the quality of the poems speak for themselves. ■

Team Albuquerque
We Teach
Written and performed by Hakim Bellamy, Carlos Contreras, Cuffee, and Kenn Rodriguez.

We teach
teach through break-beats
paint ink and congo drums
teaching old natives
assuming positions in the roles of modern sons
so for the future of things the outlook becomes:
watch out, here we come
twenty-first century
public enemy number one

We teach
teach rhymes that preach
its intent inconsistency
occasionally intersecting
when seats and stars align in the classrooms

We teach
We don't need a bully pulpit
erected in Ms. Poster's 2nd period

We don't need no education
masquerading as mind control
indoctrination of the Goth child in the back corner
or the *moranita* in seat 8, aisle 9 near the 2nd story window
watching her days dim into darkness

Christi's mind illuminates like lighthouse ignitions
she bright shines perfect
burning slow like tire fires
or supernovas
like a pile of gold stars on the last day of school

I have seen these things in her writing
See, scribbled blue ink on yellow legal pads
has never seemed so tragic
and I know, I should take her words seriously

She wrote,
"Dad hurts my life
makes my soul black
and everything becomes pain
at six I learned the best places to hide
at nine that I could take it out on the kids at school
at thirteen that all my teachers are as fucked as my dad
I am dark, dying, and not worth it"

But in poetry class, Christi bright shines perfect
She's taught me lessons I never knew I should learn
I want to tell her she deserves to have the word Everlast tattooed on her heart
that to live through what she has would keep me in my best hiding places for
lifetimes
Christi bright shines perfect
I will always take her words seriously

and it seems like our children are afraid of the dark these days
and we call these dark days nights
that depletion of energy that takes a lifetime of replenishing
diminishes their bright light but can't put it out
and the lessons we've learned from the abused youth
have become too numerous to count
no church figures or media image
can sexually violate or hate that knowledge out
erase or block that knowledge out
'cause parents prosecute while kids forgive
parents complain while kids laugh and live
even in the face of hate
even after the baddest and darkest days

they give praise with the way they play
give blessings when they show real concern
rather than feigned interest when they say:
"Mommy, how was your day?"
"Daddy, why are you crying?"

I tell them, 'cause you taught me that it's okay to cry
when something's worth crying over
and I'm learning to cry
over you
No relief from puffy eyes and lost sleep
we weep until we're weak for weeks
like we can't see through the mad dog's masking, stone-washed opticals
and teenage broken bodies
laid up in hospitals
We can change that
Teachers seem like constables on guilty before innocent orders
but we can change that
show students that education systems aren't prisons
We can change that

They are prisms to crystallize
the multiple manners with which we reach for the stars
and teach teachers to preach
pure learning
not lesson plans

Now class,
what have we learned today? ▪

Figure 3. Team Albuquerque on
the Finals Stage at NPS 2005.
Courtesy of David Huang

Team Charlotte

Two Minutes

Written by Boris "Bluz" Rogers; performed by Maze Forever, Q, Bluz, Mekkah, and Queen Sheba.

She stopped breathing
about two minutes ago.
She exhaled the last bit of fight she had left
about two minutes ago
on a cold, hard, wooden floor,
next to a shattered picture of her children,
who hide inside a closet,
muffling tears as they listen,
listen to their mother whimpering,
bloody, swollen lips whispering messages to God:
"Please watch over them."
She fights through the pain of broken ribs and punctured lung
to say it again, to make sure God is still listening:
"Please, watch over them."
As her one good eye sheds tears mixed with blood,
she is looking in their direction.
She prays for their protection,
because when you're ten,
it's hard to understand the image of love
in the mirror when this is its reflection.
It's hard to understand the safety of love
when this is its protection.
It's hard to follow your heart
when this is its tragic path and deadly direction
because daddy is leading the way
as head of household,
and right now his bloody fists
are in control of an emotional dictatorship
and they are making aggressive decisions
that place mommy in fear position
and the children listen,
wishing Mommy wouldn't voice her opinion because,

"please, not like this
not in front of the children"
seems to only add to the campaign of rage and adrenaline.
Votes are in.
Nose is broken,
Jawbone unhinged,
a left arm will probably never see their smiling faces again.
The breathing is growing thin,
and through it all,
the children are listening,
listening to their mother dying
at the hands of a man that vowed to love her,
hands that used to softly touch her
and strong arms that would stretch out wide and gently hug her.
These same hands now choke and slug her.
Tattooed arms with her name and love intertwined like a vine
push and shove her
until she falls and cracks her spine.
She's lying on a cold, hardwood floor trying to breathe.
"Come on girl, get up"
and fight.
"Get him off you,
grab the kids and run"
and breathe.
"Oh god
it in you,
just get your hands up"
and fight.
"Please, God, make him stop."
Breathe.
As she stopped breathing about two minutes ago
staring into the eyes of her children with lips whispering messages to God,
"Please watch over them,"
she didn't ask forgiveness of her sins.
She only asked,
"Please, god, watch over them."

Team Ft. Worth

In Our Heaven

Written and performed by Janean Livingston, Chuck Jackson, and Michael Guinn.

There's a darkness still bleeding from this wound,
because where I'm from
has become a place without drums for children
just slums in need of rebuilding.

The ghetto

In our heaven
there are no streets of gold
or angels standing at crystal podiums
waiting to greet you at the pearly gates.
There are no harps or rainbows or grand pianos,
nothing beautiful
and maybe this . . . is why children
hoping for better tomorrows
keep slippin' through the cracks.

In our heaven
you just step through a hole in a barbed-wire fence
leading to an empty playground
where dead pygmies hang from monkey bars
like little potbellied bats
whose wings have been clipped by an angry god
too busy to answer prayers.

Near the entrance, there's a giant dumpster
overflowing with the bad experiments of abandoned babies
screaming for their teenage mothers,
and I suppose that's where lost souls go.

Inside, a man wearing an "I love Bush" T-shirt
smiles like a pimp

as he checks his list for section 8 rape
and motions to a rickety wooden ladder
where drug dealers circle and grin.

In the courtyard, Billie Holiday sits
beneath a hanging tree
with noose-shaped leaves
clutching an empty syringe,
dying . . . from spiritual laryngitis.

To my left, Martin stands barefoot,
handcuffed,
surrounded by confederate soldiers yelling,
"Ain't no dreams here, NIGGAH.
You took the wrong DAMN turn at the mountain."

To my right, the Klan rapes Abe Lincoln,
Malcom's on his back in a straitjacket, and
James Byrd is still running behind that damned truck
in Jasper, Texas,
struggling to pick up the pieces of his soul.

In our heaven
the police play paintball with the blood of black children
while Osama and Jeffrey Dahmer place bets
and the ancestors just sit on stumps like black leprechauns,
watching as priest-turned-pedophiles drool
as they wait for lil Hansels and Gretels to lose their way,
and history makes damn sure they do
by leaving trails of broken promises
scattered from the restless remains
of a million slaves.
In our heaven

the bombing of the 16th Street Baptist Church
is a national celebration,

where heroes like Hitler and Hoover
propose a toast to the ghosts of dead daughters
and anyone caught believing themselves—
ANYONE—
would have their spirits lynched
by the rope of their own hope

'cause in our heaven
it's a sin to dream!
Foster homes become concentration camps for children
starving for attention,
and there ain't no such thing as college
because knowledge is not the key to success,
and HERE they don't give a damn if you don't do your best
because it don't matter.
This don't matter.
We don't matter.
You see,
THIS is what we see in our heaven,
and if things don't change,
this is all we'll BE in our heaven.

This is what we believe our heaven to be,
'cause in our heaven
there is no tomorrow . . .
just the hell of living today. ▪

Figure 4. Team Ft. Worth on
the Finals Stage at NPS 2005.
Courtesy of David Huang

Team Hollywood
The Spark
Written by Ratpack Slim; performed by Ratpack Slim and Simply Cat.

this
is the spark.
this is the
onyourmarkgetsetGO
that launches me outta my seat
and makes me attack my keyboard
or rip open my notebook
(being extra careful of course because it's falling apart and held together
with rubber bands)
but this is the beginning of an inspiring idea
that was inspired by an idea.
this is the energy of seeing something amazing
and just basking in its
amazocity
instead of saying
"i can do that better"
say
"i can do that"
and better words have never been spoken
but never say never
so i keep on trying to hit the set of syllables just so
and just so i can share
with anyone who will listen.

and right now
today
what i want to talk about
is the goddamn spark.

it's the eclectic electric elective ingested by the collective
for purposes of education, entertainment, or enlightenment
it's the feeling you get when you hear some really tight shit!

it's the feeling that makes your whole body tense up with
jubilation.
it's the kind of revelation
that makes you say
that's right
or
tell it, child.
it's the click you get when you listen to the first dj shadow record.
it's the click that makes you wanna
dance
wanna rhyme
wanna laugh
wanna cry
wanna nod
wanna fuck
wanna be all you can be
(in the most non-armed forces sense of the term).

this is the feeling you get
when you see your favorite singer live and onstage
and you are crushed up against the amp
and the dude next to you is sweaty and smells like ass
but you don't care
because you get a chance to see
the spark
which was the by-product of a spark
which was most likely the by-product of another spark
unless that was a blatant rip-off
but you know what?
even justin timberlake is still super sparky.

this is the feeling that is butterfly in nature.
this is the shit that changes your nomenclature.
these are the relations you can really relate to.
this is the fuckin' spark!

it's the jump-start to your battery when you're stalled on the 101.
the goose to your spiritual derriere
the locus for your next opus
this is the focus for exploding psychosis.
these are the brownies from alice b. toklas.
this is the fuckin' spark!

this is getting geeked off of positive energy.
these are vibes talented friends are sending me.
this is the reflection of the best of me.
and i pray
i give you the recipe
for
the spark. ▪

Chapter Two

Making a Scene, 1990–1994

"Isn't there supposed to be a reading here in about twenty minutes?"
I asked . . . "It was cancelled," the bartender said. "With all that slop
out there today, there wouldn't have been much point to it. Poetry's a
beautiful thing, but it's hardly worth freezing your ass off for."
                                            —Paul Auster, Leviathan

Slam first made its way into the poetry scene in Albuquerque
in the mid-1990s. Before the first slam in 1994, the poetry
scene in Albuquerque was being revitalized by innovative
poets like Lisa Gill, Juliette Torrez, and Mitch Rayes. New
ideas and creative interaction with audience energized the
local scene and whipped up the chaos that led to Slam's
emergence and quick evolution.

At its root, stem, and flower, Slam is inclusive in a way
that is unique among modern performance. Poetry Slam
audiences (and indeed slammers themselves) constitute a
diversity of age, gender, race, and sexual orientation that is
resoundingly absent in the audiences found at opera, hip-
hop concerts, repertory theatre, traditional poetry readings,
and other performing arts events. Inclusiveness and aggres-
sive community involvement have been the cornerstones of
the success of Poetry Slam in Albuquerque and across the
country. From the first Albuquerque Poetry Slam in 1995 to
the National Poetry Slam in 2005, the audience for poetry and
the number of poets has increased steadily.

Part of the magic and power of Slam comes from the
transformative moment of connection between poet and
audience born of practiced, rigorous, intentional, and honed

performance. A poet—through excellent writing, superlative performance, and an unflagging dedication to both—can achieve oneness with an audience in the space of about 180 seconds. Performance is the bridge that provides an undeniable, unmistakable, momentarily unbreakable connection between poet, audience, poem, shared emotion, message, and story.

This moment plays out in almost any slam. Almost weekly throughout the year in Albuquerque, for the last ten years, this magic has taken place in some bar or coffee shop or local venue. This book tries to capture and communicate some of those moments of time, those confluences of people and place and poetry, such as that one night at the Fabulous Dingo Bar when slam poet Traci Paris stopped time and pulled an audience into her experience with words. These moments, piling up on each other, illuminate the relationship between the people who have worked long and diligently to create and grow the Albuquerque poetry scene and the community they serve.

The poets who helped Slam and a new generation of poetry and poets take root and grow in Albuquerque did not content themselves to read and compete in bars and coffeehouses. They took their words to elementary, middle, and high schools; senior centers; street corners (a.k.a. drive-by poetry); and incarceration centers, mostly receiving no compensation for their time or art other than appreciation. These poets were digging their poetic fingers into the rich loam of this new art form called Poetry Slam, creating something vital and vibrant and rude and insistent, something that transcends stolid, comfortable writing and sing-song la la la laaa performance that poets until then had become known for. This new art form makes young people want to write poetry, read poetry, go to poetry readings, and yes (GASP) Slam. These slam poets have the fervor of missionaries whose only god is the word written and spoken, whose only commandments are listen, feel, understand, and know that you too can write and speak this way—that your voice matters. Slam is one of the most effective tools around for engaging young people in the art and craft of poetry.

Although many poets would appear, rise to local fame, and eventually move on, there were a few who began to lay the groundwork for a lasting network of support and ties to the larger community. A trio of men, in particular, individually and together set the stage for others to share. Homegrown poet Kenn Rodriguez, Texas-import-via-Boston Slam Team Champion Danny Solis, and Colorado-transplant-that-grows-better-in-New-Mexico Don McIver have consistently represented the best of Slam to Albuquerque, constantly making room for others, opening doors that allowed performance to infiltrate other spheres. Through their dedication and hard work, Slam has risen from a marginal and novelty side act to the main show in town. ■

Mitch Rayes

Albuquerque Poetry Scene, 1990–1994

Poet, organizer, and musician, Mitch Rayes was a cofounder of Flaming Tongues, Inc.

In 1990 you could still hear live poetry at three campus-area bookstores, usually published poets on a book tour. There was the occasional university event, and there were private gatherings. When Lisa Harris started hosting a weekly open mic at E. J.'s Coffeehouse, the core of what was to become the Albuquerque new wave got its first steady venue. The energy was intense and contagious, and before long, we were packing the joint.

In late 1992 Jim Reilly started Poetry & Beer at Beyond Ordinary and moved it quickly over to the Fabulous Dingo Bar. Now we had a monthly bar reading, and a feedback loop was activated that remains unbroken to this day: POETS—feed—AUDIENCES—feed—POETS. Venues began to take notice, and by 1994 there were twenty or more. The situation began to reach critical mass.

Juliette Torrez had spent the summer that year organizing spoken word for Lollapalooza coast to coast, and she came back determined to put Albuquerque on the national map. She had also decided that Albuquerque audiences were ready to pay money for good poetry. Her trademark feature showcases, usually coupled with a worthy cause, were groundbreaking successes. In the fall of 1994 she also put on the very first slam in the state of New Mexico at Jack's Lounge (won by the late Trinidad Sanchez Jr.). Soon Poetry & Beer had incorporated a monthly slam, and in the spring of 1995, Albuquerque had its first Slam team.

Lisa Gill (another Lollapalooza veteran) was by then no longer waiting for dates with audiences. She had begun ambushing them at bus stops with drive-by readings and in bars and restaurants with trays of poetry "kisses." Her guerilla army was called the Local Poets Guild, and we all had a number. Poems began popping up on light posts and in phone booths. This was when she conceived the first Poets' Diner, now an international franchise.

In the fall of 1995, Lisa, Juliette, and I formed Flaming Tongues, Inc., which would be the umbrella organization for slams, festivals, and a multitude of other projects over the next several years. I started a monthly newsletter, *The Tongue*, to try and inform the various factions and their constituencies in the now exploding scene. It ran for eight years, and I felt lucky to cover even one third of what was actually out there. Juliette proposed we do a poetry festival, and we produced four in a row from 1996 to 1999, featuring over three hundred poets from across the country, with a combined attendance around ten thousand. The feedback loop had now expanded nationally. Albuquerque was on the map, and Albuquerque audiences were ready for anything we could bring them.

The team that brought the 2005 National Slam Championships to Albuquerque is the best we've ever had. Its members have all impacted this scene individually, as both artists and as organizers; many go back to the beginning.

Of course, none of it would be possible without the hundreds of poets who have made this scene what it is. The most supportive community anywhere continues to grow. ▪

Mitch Rayes
Coyote

A man tries
to stand up straight,

a stupid man, a genius.
Stripped, whittled
to dust it's true
that we lose
the hands we once had,
the faces we've worn, the hearts
we tried out—

and yet we remain, proud
fools:
those who believe in people
before poems, others
in a legend made
entirely of words.

But the world will be different
because we have lived.

In the final light
of the longest day, the bleached
bones of these vain things:

a bag of poems bought
with our own honest sweat,
and a string of crushed hearts
no one could lift up. ▪

Lisa Gill
The Wind

has taken my breath
and lodged it in a high rock crevice
a place meant for birds

I don't have a keeled breastbone
I have vertigo
and a desire to overtake my body

on the ascent
the sun dries my face faster than I weep
so perhaps I am not sad

here where vision is a long tumble
and my hands and knees know rock
and trembling

what am I but head and torso
some arms and legs
another glyph of tortoise or lizard

a person carved into longing
below
I find a white bed

someone wept
or something flowed
this too must be tasted

the crystals are not salt
I could crawl under cover of gypsum
let the chambers of my heart fill

with silt some glossy agates
already rocks are risen like vertebrae
and vertebrae are imbedded in rock

I climb again
this time to the mesozoic
run my fingers over rock faces

press my tongue to a dinosaur bone
my mouth is this old
sand shifts in the corners of my lips

within centuries I too will be worn smooth
with my bones sheered off and scattered
everything is exposed to what the wind can carry

look at this gaping
arroyos within ravines within gorges
time twisting

tunneling back
through caves of mud
caves of granite

caves with a single rusted tin can
and entrances so narrow I slide on my belly
like a snake slither over sandstone

find refuge
in this place where everything is hard pressed—
Ojito, I have walked on blood

and seen the earth crack wide open
to spill a few birds
and a bit of water ■

Figure 5. Lisa Gill during
Day Events at NPS 2005.
Courtesy of David Huang

Juliette Torrez
Albuquerque

as i drive down albuquerque streets
edges of houses pop out of gray sky
undisguised by barren trees
twenty-three shades of brown
stucco painted to look like adobe
we're driving past, past the porches
where strings of red chile
hung there in welcome
how now brown town?
and it's good to be here
though when I'm gone
i don't miss you much
i even dogged you, albuquerque
because you are
a hard-hearted town
dressed in fake mud
being something you're not
personality split by two sides of the city
uptown and downtown, the heights and the valley
split by the businessmen
developing their property
you never had a good image of yourself,
Albuquerque
you don't love yourself the way
san francisco loves itself
the way seattle loves itself
the way santa fe loves itself
and i wonder what crime
stained these hills
that made you such a hard-hearted town
dressed in brown
ribboned in interstate asphalt

and a poisoned river
i'm fascinated by your sinister side,
albuquerque
and pray you don't claim me
as a blood sacrifice
but when i come back
i see the way the sunset hits the sandias
and remember what it was
that i miss about this town
i see the morning light bright blue
and remember what i miss
about this town
and when i go to the frontier restaurant
and ask for a green chile burger
they know exactly what it is
and they give it to me
and I remember what I miss
about this town
albuquerque
i love you i hate you
i'll always come back to you
the land of entrapment
a curse or a blessing
i don't know the answer
i just keep returning ▧

Poetry Slam, Inc. and Susan McAllister

*Slam Poetry Demystified**

Poetry Slam is the competitive art of performance poetry. Established in Chicago in the mid-1980s, Slam began as a uniquely American genre, which has evolved into an international art form emphasizing poetic excellence and audience involvement.

The poetry: Slam emphasizes both writing and performance, encouraging poets to focus on what they say as well as how they say it. It is living poetry, with deep roots and many branches. At any given slam, the audience may experience love poems, revolution poems, confessional, tragic, or comic poems. Poetry Slam serves as the forum for a remarkable variety of our most eloquent poets, social critics, and chroniclers of the human condition. These poets are of all ages and backgrounds: high school students and teachers; doctors, construction workers, clerks, college freshmen, and PhDs; truckers, librarians, homemakers, and plumbers.

The audience: Poetry Slam was started as an attempt by poet Marc Smith ("So What!") to revive and revitalize interest in poetry readings; he wanted to build audiences and expand the public's perception of poetry. Slam encourages audiences because it asks them to become part of the experience, to interact by responding to the poem, and the performance. In some cases, particularly with well-known poems, the audience response becomes part of the poem. Even newcomers to poetry find themselves swept up in the performance; there is no such thing as passive listening at a slam.

The competition: Poetry Slams are competitions that follow basic rules instituted by the national governing organization Poetry Slam, Inc. (PSi). Poets perform their original work and are scored by five judges selected randomly from the audience. The judges are provided with specific criteria and are as diverse as the poets they score. The poets compete in round-robin matches with the highest scoring poets proceeding to the next round until a winner emerges. In Albuquerque, the winner of each individual slam is qualified to compete in the Grand Slam at the end of the year. The four top-scoring poets from the Grand Slam constitute the team sent to the national finals. At this time, almost every state sends a team; some states send more than one. Slam is beginning to see participation by Canadian and European teams as well. The National Slams have been held every year since 1990, when they began with two teams, San Francisco and Chicago. In 2003 there were sixty-three teams competing in the national championship, held that year in Chicago. In 2005, seventy-five teams competed in the Nationals in Albuquerque. ■

---

*Adapted with permission from PSi website: http://www.poetryslam.com/

Robert Wilson

First Slam at Jack's Lounge

Doctor, poet, writer of short stories, accessible sage, supportive and generous honorary father-figure of the early Slam scene, Dr. Bob was a member of the first and second Albuquerque Slam teams.

1994. What is it, September? A Tuesday night, I think, at Jack's Lounge—a drop-in on Central for grad students and secret lovers, salesmen, lawyers, boozers, and losers. A dark bar—big mirror behind all the lit up liquor bottles. What anyone says here is nobody else's business. Until tonight.

The poets and a small scattered poet's audience filter in around eight. Someone has brought a mic and speakers, Mitch Rayes, probably—troubadour/minstrel/poet—family man and forever friend. Or Kenn Rodriguez—long, long hair—headbanger inside the soft heart of a people's poet. Or Juliette Torrez, who does everything—forty phone calls in forty minutes—and published the first ever blood-splattered chapbook. And then Matt—Matthew John Conley—the brilliant mouth, the Mohawk, the man in and of the moment. And Jim Stewart, latter-day lizard king, majoring in self-dissection, minoring in self-loathing. And Lisa Gill, whose spoken word inhabits the space between sex and the metaphysics of the psyche. And Trinidad Sanchez Jr., the sojourner from the South who knows twice as much as all of us. And me, a spoken word virgin.

There are other poets at Jack's this night of Albuquerque's inaugural Slam season. One or more of the Bobs? Swearingen, Monson, Reeves? Maybe (Lord) Henry Harrison? If not then, then soon thereafter: Tamara Nicholl, Traci Paris, and that guy who channeled Kurt Cobain.

The voices, distinct and emphatic, hold Jack's captive. Captivated? Not necessarily. The nature of Slam is uncertainty. Unpredictability. The convergence of poets and their voices, audience and their ears, judges and their zero-to-ten, is just a momentary, unrehearsed realignment of the chaos. Slam is an antiproduction, in its essence best suited for places like Jack's.

And so, to all the places like Jack's, all the bars and coffeehouses that opened their doors and floors to performing poets, all the places that offered up their clientele, the poets say, "Thank you." ▪

Robert Wilson
Drought

I've heard this story before.
It's the one where he stops coming home, after work
until it's very, very late
and you don't know where he goes.
It's the one where he's not talking
and you don't know what's going on.
The one where he says nothing's wrong
and you've lost the fifteen pounds
you've always wanted to lose and
it was easy this time because you just can't eat.
And no matter what you do you
can't get warm. And you haven't had sex for six
weeks and he still says nothing's wrong.
It's the one where suddenly he says he's leaving
and finally he's talking, but his mind's made up.
And then he doesn't want to talk anymore
because his mind's made up
and you still don't know why he's leaving.
It's the one where he says he'll stay until July
and it feels so strange with him lying
there next to you, and you don't know why
he can't just sleep on the couch
if his mind's made up about not wanting
any part of you
for the rest of his life.
It's the one where the kids are too quiet
like they know something's coming
but they don't know what because he's
not talking and you're just waiting
to see if he's really going to leave
or if maybe he'll get it out of his system
and come to his senses
so you won't have to tell them—shrivel them up
like seedlings barely out of the ground
in a drought that won't let up
under a sky that won't let down
and you just keep waiting, hoping,
aching for rain. ■

Bob Swearingen
Blue Plate Special

Friday settled like ambergris
on Central Avenue

bazooka exhaust and sunlight
mixed in a traffic cocktail
of big city swamp gas

joggers plodded
oblivious to Molotov
backfires of failing metal

wise old street boys
walked slowly
barely breathing
an emphysemic elixir
from coupe de villes
and gas *du jours*
mixed with a fine
oil slick vinaigrette

the dead man on the street
was a problem

so ambulance people
sopped him up
they were breadsticks
in this meal
sinew, bone, and blood
the *entrée*

just above
a crow swam through
the Galliano air to
a drunken landing
on a cable TV wire
and demanded
better programming

eleven hours later
a curtain fell
to starry winks
over black velveteen

and everybody

came out

for a bow

Trinidad Sanchez Jr.
Chinco de Mayo

The *Denver Post* in the state of Colorado
states Chinco de Mayo is more popular,
because it is easier to say than
diez y seis de septiembre!
We know, Chinco de Mayo is popular because
Chinco de Mayo is 350,000 brown people.
Chinco de Mayo is Mexican mariachi and beer.
Mexican music and beer. Mexican food and beer.
Mexican art and beer. Hispanics and beer.
Chicanos and beer. Latinos and beer.
Lowriders and beer. Carnivals and beer.
Parades and beer. Adults and beer.
Rides and beer. Beer and beer.
"Some of us stay home because
there are too many *borrachos* on the road."
"All other events have beer
the Irish drink beer on St. Patrick's Day,
he—was Catholic, the pope is Catholic
this negative, cynical rap isn't given to them.
Everyone else can drink beer but we can't."
Selling beer is another way for beer companies
to do their "initiatives" in the community.
An opportunity for them "to be out" in the community—
"TO SELL THEIR PRODUCTS!" I mean beer.
Besides, Coors spent $50 thousand on this Chinco
and promises to spend another $50 thousand later.
Gracias a Dios, politicians are protecting our rights
to drink beer on Chinco de Mayo and protecting our *dinero*.
If 350,000 brown people drink an average of three beers each
at $4.00 a pop, which is more than the $50 thousand Chincos
they spent on the Chicano this year,
and more than the $50 thousand promised.
Can you add it all up, Brown America?
Corporate America, she knows Latinos have buying power—
400 billion worth! Why in Nashville, Tennessee,
Chinco de Mayo is bigger and better . . . like the *jalapeños*

growing bigger and hotter year after year in our garden.
Black People, African Americans, don't feel sad.
Corporate America will not be outdone by Chicanos.
They promise to spend the same amount of Chincos
in your community and sell the same amount of beer.

Coors and Budweiser know . . .
What is a Black celebration without chitlins and beer?
Bean pie and beer. Jazz and beer. Rap and beer.
Black/afrikan art and beer. Blues and Beer.
U.S. Dept. of Health and Human Services research
states in bold black print in the *Denver Post*,
"Young Hispanics are more likely to drink and get drunk"
at an earlier age than non-Hispanics.
That's okay as long as they are drinking
Coors and Budweiser.
This year, like last year, more and more
Mexicans are waving their flags,
telling us they are more Mexican than a Fox,
more Mexican than their mothers,
more Mexican than the *águila mejicana*,
more Mexican than the flags they are waving,
certainly they are more Mexican
than the thousands of barrels of Coors & Budweiser
they drink every year.
This year, *el profesor*, reminds us of the truth,
the lesson—*la mera verdad* of Chinco de Mayo is . . .
we have to resist the bottled oppression,
because beer companies . . . *hijos de su tiznada*
know their brand of oppression, when it comes in a bottle,
is more easily swallowed in the Chicano community.
Beer Companies don't give a Chinco about resisting oppression.
They will bottle it and take our hard earned Chincos
and smile all the way to the bank . . .
"Yo soy Chicano tengo calor
americano, pero con honor
cuando me dicen, que hay revolución
defiendo mi raza con mucho amor." ■

Chinco De Mayo

El *Denver Post* en el estado de Colorado
declara "El Chinco de Mayo" es más popular
porque es más fácil decir que el
Diez y Seis de Septiembre!
Sabemos que Chinco de Mayo es popular porque .
Chinco de Mayo es 350,000 gente de color bronce,
Chinco de Mayo es Mariachi mexicana y cerveza.
Música mexicana y cerveza. Comida mexicana y cerveza.
Arte mexicana y cerveza. Hispanos y cerveza.
Chicanos y cerveza. Latinos y cerveza.
Lowriders y cerveza. Carnavales y cerveza.
Fiestas y cerveza. Adultos y cerveza.
Juegos y cerveza. Cerveza y cerveza.
"Algunos de nosotros quedemos en casa
porque hay mucho borrachos en las calles."
"Hay cerveza en todas las otras fiestas,
los irlandeses toman cerveza Día de San Patricio—
él era católico, el Papa es católico
estas quejas cínicas no se dan a ellos.
Todo el mundo puede tomar cerveza menos nosotros."
Vendiendo cerveza es otra manera para que los negociantes de cerveza
hacen sus "iniciativos" en la comunidad.
Este es una oportunidad para ellos de "entrar a nuestra comunidad"
"PARA VENDER SUS PRODUCTOS." Cerveza. Quiero decir
Además, Coors gasto $50 mil en este Chinco
y prometa de gastar otro $50 mil más en el futuro."
Gracias a Dios, los políticos están protegiendo nuestro derecho
a tomar cerveza este Chinco de mayo y protegiendo nuestro dinero.
Si 350,000 gente de color toman un por medio de tres cervezas cada uno
a $4.00 pesos cada cerveza, esto es más que los $50 mil chincos
que gastan en los Chicanos este año
y más que los $50, mil prometido.
¿Raza Bronce, pueden sumar todo esto?
Por que América Negociante conoce el poder de compras de los Latinos
400 billiones en total! Fíjanse, en Nashville, Tennessee,
el Chinco de Mayo es más grande y mejor . . . como los jalapeños

creciendo más grande y más caliente año tras año en nuestro jardín.
Raza negra, americanos africanos no se sienten triste,
America Negociante no se deja rajar por los Chicanos
ellos prometan de gastar lo mismo chincos en sus comunidades
y vender el mismo cantidad de cerveza.

Coors y Budweiser saben bien . . .
¿Que es una celebración de raza negra sin chitlins y cerveza?
Pastel de fríjol y cerveza. Jazz y cerveza. Rap y cerveza.
Arte de la raza negra y africano y cerveza. Blues y cerveza.
Salud y Servicios Humanos—Los estudios del Dept. de E.U.
declara en molde negra en *el Denver Post*
"Los hispanos jóvenes son más disponibles a tomar y emborracharse"
en un edad más joven que los no Hispanos
pero esto está bien no más que están tomando
Coors y Budweiser.
Este año como el año pasado, más y más
Mejicanos están ondeado sus banderas,
declarando que son más Mexicano que un Fox
más Mexicano que sus madres,
más Mexicano que la águila mejicana,
más Mexicano que las banderas que están ondeado,
por cierto son más mejicanos,
que los miles de barriles de Coors y Budweiser
que toman cada año.
Este año el profesor, nos recordó de la verdad,
la mera neta de la lección de Chinco de Mayo es . . .
tenemos que resistir la opresión embotellado
por que las compañías de cerveza . . . hijos de su tiznada
saben bien que su tipo de opresión, cuando esta embotallada,
se traga más fácil, en la comunidad
Cerverserias no pueden molestarse un Chinco sobre la resistencia del opresión
lo van a embotallar y llevar nuestros Chincos ganado con dificultad
y sonreí de todo el camino al banco . . .
"Yo soy Chicano tengo calor
Americano pero con honor
cuando me dicen que hay revolución
defiendo mi raza con mucho amor." ▪

Enrique Harrison

Be my pearl jam
be my alice and chains, my alice in lace and whiskey for ancient sailors
light up the town with your kisses of strawberry sunsets
and smell of musk between the center of your skin
the moon for the muse
softly calling alice
softly
softly in lace leathers and chains ▪

Don McIver

Venues—Best Price Books and Coffee

A resilient builder, Don McIver creates what he wants to achieve. He finally made it onto an Albuquerque Slam Team in 2002 and became grassroots media guru for NPS 2005. He is the under-the-radar strategist, networker, smoother of egos, the calm but spinning center of the storm that is ABQ Slam. He founded Don McIver and Friends, which morphed into Blue Dragon Poetry Slam. He is the current host of Spoken Word Hour *and producer of other radio shows on KUNM.*

Best Price Books and Coffee wasn't much of a coffee shop—just a couple varieties of coffee, a bad espresso the grumpy counter staff made grudgingly, a less-than-frothy cappuccino, and the usual assortment of cheap teas, if you even bothered to get someone's attention. The emphasis wasn't coffee. Unfortunately, the emphasis wasn't on books either. Put more on the shelf as some sort of decoration, books were sold if at all to the occasional book collector who wanted out-of-date textbooks, collections of bad poetry, and first editions of fiction that never made it to paperback because no one bought the hardback. But Best Price Books and Coffee made up for its shortcomings by being long on atmosphere. Oh, it had atmosphere: small round tables that wobbled and looked out onto the freak show of Central Avenue, beat-up old chairs tucked into corners or behind bookshelves, and in the summer, an outdoor patio that became the hangout for transient teenagers. Except Sundays.

On Sundays, a staple of ten regulars and other assorted poets would descend on Best Price for the weekly poetry open mic hosted by Kenn Rodriguez. In cold weather, we'd take up the table in the back room and stand up from where we were sitting to read to the other poets. In warm weather, we'd be out on the patio, with the PA pointed to the street. One night, Kenn read an opening poem, and one of the people walking by decided to stop and check it out. As Kenn finished, the guy heckled him, finishing with, "Speak English. You're in America."

This didn't settle well with Kenn, and he started talking to the guy from the microphone. Names were exchanged. Cultural insults ensued, and the next thing I know, I'm talking to Kenn on the corner of Central and University trying to calm him down as he's yelling up Central, "I'm right here, motherfucker. Right here."

That was Slam at Best Price Books and Coffee. ■

Kenn Rodriguez
The Anatomy of a History Lesson

Every time someone
yells "Speak english, this is America,"

I feel like dropping some
knowledge on them.

I feel like dropping more than knowledge
on their pointy, bigoted heads.

I feel like dropping a fist,
but I know history is a ton of bricks

better suited for those ignorant fools.
I feel like saying, "This is New Mexico,

which was stolen from Mexico by America,
so you should be speaking *español*,"

amigo.

But I know that history lessons
are stunted & misshapen,
waterlogged with lies.

I know I should be saying,
"You're in New Mexico, which was stolen

from Mexico by 'America,' which was stolen
from the 'Indians' by the 'Spanish,'"

but that's like saying my belly button
was stolen from my legs by my chest, which was
stolen from my head by my neck.

It's like saying my left hand was stolen
from my wrist by my arm,

which was acting in accordance
to the imperial rule of my shoulder.

It's like saying my thoughts were stolen
from my brain by my mind, which was stolen

from my psyche by my soul,
which is to say, it's all the part of the one,

but I still want to teach these *pendejos*
something other than the Treaty of Guadalupe Whoop-ass,

my own Mexican-American War of 1998,
which is at an impasse

when this stringy-haired, blond, blue-eyed bigot
says,

"I should go over there & kick all your
Spanish-speaking asses."

I know he's no Davy Crockett
& I'm no General Santa Anna.

He's no General Pershing &
I ain't no Pancho Villa

& this sure ain't the Alamo
or Columbus, New Mexico.

Instead I close my eyes, see
a dark-skinned warrior with a Spanish surname

crinkling between his broad shoulders
as he swats lily-white baseballs

over the Wrigley Field fence,
four in one weekend, & say to myself,

Take that, Manifest Destiny.
Take that, General Zachary Taylor.

Take that, Republic of Texas.
Take that, America,

but I know it's a charade.
I know he could hit 100 home runs &

it would do nothing to right the wrongs,
replace the king & the queen or pawns

on the board of the western hemisphere.
I am not part of the solution.

I am part of the problem,
which is made of the parts of my body

that tried to colonize each other
earlier in this poem

& in my mind's eye,
which was stolen from my memories,

stolen from my life,
stolen from the cosmos itself.

I can see the same ignorant, inebriated idiot
striding up to Sammy Sosa,

who has just broken through the barrier
Maris and the Babe tore through,

& rather than shaking his hand
or congratulating him,

this "patriot" reduces his open hand into
a pointing finger & screams,

"Speak english, this is America." ▪

Daniel S. Solis

Taos Poetry Circus

The Taos Poetry Circus began somewhere in the mists of another time, when New Mexico and Taos were different places, with fewer people and more magic, when spirit animals, luminous and ephemeral, were as common as elk or magpies are today.

Anne MacNaughton and Peter Rabbit dreamed a dream of poets converging from lands both real and mythical, so they cast a mighty spell up in the mountains to the north. For days, heat lightning crashed the mountainsides. The stars stopped and pondered this, and the moon put her chin in her hands and wondered at the thunder and the crackling light. For as many days as the lightning, there came rain, heavy torrents and whispering drizzles, raindrops, fat as globs of oatmeal and thin as needles. For as many days as rain fell, there came fog and mists and winds that meandered and moaned, that swirled in the arroyos and chanted in ancient kivas.

After all these days of rain and mist, wind and lightning, the sun came out to see what was what. What he saw was a new gathering of poets and would-be poets, of bards, minstrels, and fakers, of coyotes and crows, bears and jaguars and owls, of mystics and mages, monks and mercenaries, of seers, singers, and spinners of webs of stories, a gathering the likes of which had not been seen in many ages. The sun said, "This is good. I will shine on this thing and make it warm, and it will grow." And so it was.

In its twenty years of existence between 1982 and 2003, the Taos Poetry Circus brought world-class poets to Taos, New Mexico, for a weekend poetry festival. The Taos Poetry Circus crammed an incredible amount of poetry into eight days in the form of readings, workshops, question and answer sessions, open mics, slams, and, of course, the one and only, world-famous Heavyweight Poetry Bout.

It was in these "bouts" that poetic luminaries such as such as Allen Ginsberg, Patricia Smith, Ntozake Shange, Jimmy Santiago Baca, Anne Waldman, Quincy Troupe, and Sherman Alexie engaged in ten rounds of intense poetry performance that by the end often had audiences roaring with enthusiasm. These contests were staged in a makeshift boxing ring replete with ropes, a ring-girl, an old style microphone lowered on a cord to the announcer, and a bell that was rung between rounds.

Peter Rabbit could always be found in the center of the action as the bout's referee, sporting his trademark Shriners' fez. These poetic *mano-a-mano* struggles often generated controversy, which Peter Rabbit seemed to welcome, almost like a poetry P. T. Barnum adhering to the old adage: "any press is good press."

Peter Rabbit came across as a combination of the Mad Hatter, Don King, and a scuffed up, poor man's Merlin. You never knew what outrageous thing he might do or say at any given moment, and he seemed to love it that way. Anne MacNaughton, his poetry co-conspirator, by contrast always seemed cool and measured, intellectually assessing the situation and keeping things lively but in control. Both had raucous senses of humor that served them well in the conception, planning, and execution of a festival of this diversity and breadth.

The Taos Poetry Festival never backed down. It never tried to incorporate music or call itself a "storytelling" festival to lure poem-phobic audiences. It was always unabashedly, unapologetically about the poetry. No matter what the criticism, no one could ever contend that it ignored its primary function, giving as much poetry as it could to its avid audiences. It provided ample opportunities for poets with little or no literary reputation to read at open mics and, in its later years, in poetry slams. The Taos Poetry Circus was equal parts serious consideration of scholarly poetry, spectacle, breathtaking performance, sleight of hand, miracle, poetic epiphany, and orgy.

While the Heavyweight Bout was the gem and climax of the Taos Poetry Circus, very often, for me, the best moments were the quieter ones, those fresh poems read at open mics or slams, where poets weren't worried about literary reputations, where the only concerns were the next lines of poetry lovingly slaved over, where each poet was anxious to share something precious, something singular—a poem, just a poem.

New Mexico poets, poetry festivals, and poetry lovers owe the Taos Poetry Circus an unpayable debt, for it is, at least in part, on its mighty crazy shoulders we stand and reach for the future of poetry here in the desert.

The sun shone for many seasons on this gathering of madness and miracle, of song and incantation, and it did indeed grow, and shone as brightly as the stars tangled in the yellow moon's blue-black tresses. All the beings therein did cavort and frolic mightily under the smile of muse and magic alike. Then did the magic grow restless and say to the muse, "Let us go over that mountain, down into that valley, southward." And so they did.

Things became a little quieter up in the north, but Peter Rabbit and Anne MacNaughton did shine with the light of poetry wheresoever they did go, luminous in the high mountain's blue arms. Things got louder in the south, and many more fields of poems like sunflowers and wild unnameable animals did begin to grow and frolic mightily under the sun's broad smile, and so it is. ■

Daniel S. Solis

One-match Fire

A true story

And I let you drive home drunk
after that clumsy 5 a.m. kiss
and I lay in bed cursing myself
for being so selfish because I knew
you had a boyfriend
and we had already talked about just staying friends
but mostly I lay in bed cursing the wide world
for its series of unflinching machinations
that had brought me to this moment of nighttime
my arms not around you
my mouth as hungry for you as it had ever been for anything or anyone
my thirst like a slap
as I thought again of my drunken lunge toward every bit of you

But that
was a different night than the one I really want to talk about
This other one was a Friday night
and your boyfriend was out of town
and we were nervous
but we drank wine anyway
or maybe because of
and your dogs followed us out into the backyard
where I built a fire
and I felt like this was some sort of mystical, romantical test
and I built it just the way my friend Shana taught me
a one-match fire
and it actually lit
with just one match
and I was quite relieved
and never mind about the possible metaphors here,
too obvious, too cheesy, but
I was proud of my little fire
and you rolled up a wheelbarrow
full of more wood
and there was plenty of room left in the pit for more fire
and I thought, "What if I'm being too timid?

What if she's used to her boyfriend building a really big fire?"
and this little fire leaves her totally unsatisfied, and in fact, a little disappointed
So all of a sudden I am trapped, in my head, in a fire-making competition with your boyfriend,
who isn't even there,
but still stands between us like a wall
and so I begin snapping cedar branches from a nearby woodpile
and tossing them and the boards and the logs from the wheelbarrow
into the pit
trying to seem casual about everything
but I am wondering about my place in the fire competition
and I am using all my pyro-technique to make a huge, hot
but contained blaze
and the thing is so big that the dogs withdraw
and you get nervous—
not about us this time—
but about the house possibly igniting
and you hop over a smoldering hay bale to rescue an old wooden owl that has burst into flame
and I stand and stoke and stir the fire with a seven-foot iron rod I found nearby
feeling like the king of campfires
and I am tempted to question your impression of my fantastic fire skills
with pet-name-laced questions like
"Hot enough for you, monkey lips?"
"How bout that fire, grasshopper wings?"
"What do you think about my incredibly mind-blowing and obviously far,
far,
faaaaaaaaaaaaaar,
superior to your boyfriend's fire-building and tending skills now, chinchilla hips?"
But instead, we simply sit and drink more wine,
and share stories of our childhoods.
You tell of the secret swamp and the sinking mattress raft.
I tell of the Thanksgiving where my gang of cousins
beat another gang of cousins with sticks.
The fire pops and chortles, and the fire growls and crackles,
and we laugh and drink more wine and share those stories,
and we are both, still
nervous. ■

Daniel S. Solis

Venues—Gold Coast Coffeehouse

Gold Coast Coffeehouse was a low roar of a coffee, booze, poetry, and music venue. From the Goth kids sharing coffee cups and overflowing their ashtrays to the blue hairs finding themselves in the middle of poetry readings that were noisy and profanity drenched, the Gold Coast was a venue of many faces and flavors. Something outstanding was always happening or just about to happen. Wild, unpredictable energy was the order of the day and night. You never knew who might show up and rock the mic, from Daphne Gottleib to Mike Brown to Julia Delbridge to Patricia Smith to Marc Smith showing up one night and conducting a poetry slam where he twisted the rules to the point where they were unrecognizable and if you complained he would immediately question whether you were taking yourself too seriously.

When poetry started to happen at the Gold Coast during the 1997 Albuquerque Poetry Festival, there was an incredible vibe to the place and the readings. That first reading was a really intense and amazing show that was also oddly relaxed and fun, a rare combination in the world of live poetry shows. I hosted that reading and was lucky to have a very strong list of featured poets, with Joanne Dwyer and Levi Romero being the standouts.

Afterward the owners of Gold Coast approached me about doing a regular series. Being the new kid in town I offered the reading to several established Albuquerque poets, but they were all too busy or not interested, so I told the owners, "Sure, I'll do it!" So "Words on Wednesday" (an incarnation of an ancient Dallas poetry series that I hosted) lived again.

What followed was one of the most fun times I've ever had booking and hosting a poetry show. We had all kinds of poets and weren't afraid of bands or novelty acts either. We rarely had slams but when we did we tried to make them something out of the ordinary (Thanks again, Marc!). The poets were feisty and crazy and wonderful and Doug kept passing me cold beers and the house was consistently packed, yahoo!

The high-water mark for the Gold Coast Words on Wednesday series came when we had the mighty Monkey Girl herself, Beth Lissick, come in as a feature. I can't even guess how large the crowd was but I do know we had obliterated the fire codes. People were literally hanging through the windows of the building to hear Beth do her thing. She responded by giving one of the greatest performances of poetry I have ever seen. She got three encores and a standing ovation. What a night.

To me, that night said as much about Albuquerque poetry audiences as it did about Beth's talent as an artist. I think that a small seed was planted in my consciousness that night. A seed that would grow into the conviction that we, Albuquerque, could organize and host an event like a National Poetry Slam. ∎

María Leyba
Barrio Madonna

Soft-spoken but tough as nails, María Leyba has been a staunch advocate for the power of poetry in underrepresented communities, working with youth, jail inmates, and Native American elders, among others. The Albuquerque Slam community has adopted her as patron saint to lost souls who find their voices in the darkness.

I should have known
something was wrong
when last December
I was chosen to play
the part of *La Virgen*
in *La Pastorela* at the
South Broadway Culture Center.

I with two children
over nineteen years old
the perpetual sinner
living with a white man
who's not even my husband
the only link I have with Mary
is my name, María.

I forgot that I have
always been the
BARRIO MADONNA
mother of Weasel
El Vato Loco from B-13
surrogate mother to all
the homeboys from Barelas.

Last month I found
my son's name in the
Quik Quarter
in the section reserved for
New Mexico's Crime Stoppers.

He has always been
so photogenic
so handsome
now he stares at me
with his *chata* nose
much too large/flat
reminds me of the massive
Mexican Rain God—Tlaloc.

My family exclaims:

"You should be upset
because he's on the
most wanted
not worried about his looks."

I try to explain
you don't understand,

I'm the Barrio Madonna
who wants her cute little
boy back.

My son called a few weeks
ago told me he did
something really stupid
needed a fix bad
went on the wrong day
to the Plasma Center.
Lost it when he was told
he would have to wait
a few more days.
Thinking wasn't a priority
when he pulled out
a nine-inch knife
demanded money, got $100.00
Now he's a real fugitive—
a modern day Pancho Villa.
I told him what were
you thinking of?
robbing a place where
everyone knows you
they have your picture,

name, address/even
your blood type!

My fugitive son is
living on borrowed time
a black alley cat on the
run not wanting to get
caught.

His best friend's parents
entice him with free food/a
place to stay—greedily
plotting how to turn him in
wanting to collect the
Crime Stoppers reward money.

I the Barrio Madonna
silently cry/pray
light a candle
place it in the window
facing south in Barelas
to guide my son out of
DARKNESS! ▪

Matthew John Conley

Venues—Fabulous Dingo Bar

Originally from New Jersey, adopted in the early Albuquerque Slam scene as MJC, this toothy-grin, steel rod of a poet defected to Minneapolis in 1999 but came home in 2005 to win the Haiku Championship during NPS day events.

Figure 6. Matthew John Conley at the Dingo Bar. *Courtesy of Michael Hudock*

In the fall of '94, Jim Stewart & I stood on the corner of University & Central, just back from the Lollapalooza tour, realizing that the poetry scene in Albuquerque was dead. That summer while we were gone, the three readings in town had folded under scandal & infighting. Once Juliette Torrez returned, she convinced the Dingo Bar to take us in & host our shenanigans in this new form: the Poetry Slam. The Dingo Bar was the gritty upstart in a floundering bar scene, & Miguel Corrigan ran the place like an asylum for artists & those that designated themselves as such. From that stage we howled & laughed hilarious & filled those dusty streets with our voices from the window that was our backdrop. Bums, burnouts, broke down hearts embraced a needed void & kissed it open. Albuquerque Slam was born.

Matthew John Conley
Women Are Like Trees

Women are like trees, she said
Women are like trees &
Even she didn't know what she meant by that
Women are like trees
She said again & then
Planted herself in her bed &

Waited, & I stood there
In the middle of her room
Looking at her, as if
Looking out the window at her, thinking
About all the years she has spent
Gathering rings around her hips
Stretching out sexed like a cat toward the sun

& then she pulled me to her, &
Before I had spent even a minute
Laying at her feet in the shadow of her height
She said Hold me, &
Wrapping my arms around her
I felt as if I was the one
With peel-away bark skin

Ran my hands along her strangely fluid trunk
Swaying beside me, stretching out sexed
Like a cat toward the sun, & I
Could hear the wind rubbing the leaves together
Rubbing the leaves together like bodies soft & open
But there was time for the leaves yet
While my tongue picked ants off her branches

& the young bird in her nest of hair
Called to its mother
The young bird in her nest of hair
Hungry for another wet meal while beneath us
All along her feet children played hide-&-seek

The wind was blowing even harder as
Even the strongest leaves let go
To lay crumpled under the bare-footed
Joy of the children while my tongue picked
Ants off her branches the wind was blowing now
Even harder as even the strongest leaves let go &
All was weakness folding necessary weakness &

Women are like trees, she whispered
As the axe cut into her middle
Women are like trees, she whispered
As the sap flowed into the wound
Women are like trees, she whispered

As the wind swayed her back & forth along the weakness
As her branches bent down to dip into the water
As her strongest leaves lay crumpled
Beneath the bare-footed joy of the children
Women are like trees, she whispered

As the young bird in her nest of hair
Tried out its new, wet wings &
Called to its mother that
It could find a meal of its own ▪

Chapter Three

ABQ Poetry Slam Hits the Road, 1995–2005

Slam easily established itself in the Albuquerque community in 1995, and over the next ten years, poets and organizers worked to build a Slam family locally and put Albuquerque on the national Slam stage. They started by sending a team to compete in the 1995 National Poetry Slam for the first time in Ann Arbor, Michigan. Talent and luck fluctuated widely for Albuquerque teams from year to year, but always, poets were working to strengthen their community and polish their art, venue by venue, slam by slam, and poem by poem.

One of the identifying characteristics of Slam (stage) as opposed to typical poetry (page) is the importance of repetition and intense honing of craft. Poets will compete with the same poems for months—perfecting them over time. As the audience grows to know the poems, they become favorites, and fans show up expecting them, the way fans want to hear a band's hit at every concert.

Many Slam poets write in their heads, which means writing poems to perform out loud. Some never write them down, yet they come to be known for a particular poem—for years afterward. In choosing the poems to include for this anthology, many stories were told. "Remember when Kenn read 'Anatomy of a History Lesson' at Best Price Book and Coffee?" How could we forget? In this way, Slam poetry comes to participate in the community as a kind of oral history. Again and again, the magic of a particular poet, a certain poem, in that specific place on that day created a moment that was remembered and talked about for years. ■

Kenn Rodriguez

The First Nationals Team from Albuquerque

Founder and longtime host of Mas Poetry Slam, Kenn Rodriguez has been a mentor and gentle encourager of youth, sports fanatic, and repeat Albuquerque Poetry Slam Team coach. He was a member of the first ABQ National Slam Team in 1995 and first ever ABQ National Slam Team Champions in 2005.

Five twentysomethings in a red Nissan pickup with a white truck shell u-clamped to it, driving across the Midwest: That, largely, was how the first Albuquerque Poetry Slam Team got to its first National Poetry Slam in Ann Arbor, Michigan.

The two non-twentysomethings—ABQ city champ Trinidad "Trino" Sanchez Jr. and team member Dr. Bob Wilson—flew in. We other fools—Slam mistress Juliette Torrez, our manager Eric Bodwell, captain Matthew John Conley, Jim Stewart, and myself—drove in that smelly red truck through thunderstorms and road closures.

The trip to Ann Arbor largely illustrates that 1995 team—a first-year team, underdogs that came together in an unlikely way. Dr. Bob is literally a doctor. Trino was a married poet. The rest of us were just living that ne'er-do-well poet lifestyle.

NPS in 1995 still had a freak show summer camp kinda feel to it. Team ABQ fit right in. In 1995 the trip and the poetry were one and the same. Juliette and our other big organizer Mitch Rayes (who made the trip in his own truck) got us there.

Because of Juliette, we'd seen national poets in ABQ and at the SXSW (South by Southwest) Music Conference in Austin, Texas. We also had the naiveté to think we could go toe-to-toe with them. Upon seeing the likes of Danny

Solis, Crystal Williams, Wammo, and Taylor Mali, we knew we had work to do, but we truly believed that we could get to that level.

Like Eric's red truck, we didn't come away unscathed (the truck had a huge gash torn into it; the team didn't make it to the semifinals). But we got to taste the finals stage, having been asked to perform in the opening show thanks to Trino's signature poem "Let Us Stop This Madness," which we turned into a group poem.

I could go on about the trip—the humid lunch stop in Missouri, the thunderstorm through Illinois (and the stop in Funks Grove, Illinois—where Parliament/Funkadelic should retire when it's all said and done), the funky house owned by friends of Mitch's. It almost seems more important than the poetry. But it's not. It's as important, because to a person, we transformed that experience into poetry and art that would help sustain ABQ poetry for the next ten years. ■

Kenn Rodriguez
I Am

You don't know me
but you think you do

You read the nine letters
of my family name
R-O-D-R-I-G-U-E-Z, & think
you have a complete picture

But it is fractured & misleading
a jigsaw puzzle with pieces missing
that even I may never find

You think you know me
because of the color of my hair
the tone of my skin
the sound of my voice

But you don't know

You don't know that I am
the Tennessee Volunteer
racing down Grand Avenue in my '59 Chevy

The freckle-faced mountain of a man
you call *gringo, gabacho*
owner of the junkyard at the end of town
Father of seven half-breed children
living on Eleventh Street

I am
also their mother
the *Norteña Mexicana*
a generation from the fields
working in a factory in California

I am
dark skin, fierce eyebrows &
a fiercer temper

I will love you hard
with a belt across your behind
or vinegar-soaked potatoes
laid across your forehead
when you fall ill

I am
more
I am the town sheriff
El Alcalde, the town mayor
I am
also *el borracho*, the town drunk

I am
more still

I am
Spanish arrogance claiming
impossibly untainted blood
in the glaring reality that is
Nuevo Mexico

I am
oppressor and oppressed
the every likelihood of being
encased in my contradictory flesh

Hating hand of the Conquistador
conquerors of this land
the equally hating hand
of the Pueblo Indian rebel
trying in vain to reclaim the land

I am
also the land
of the potter, black as obsidian

I am
also her clay

The Son of *Nahuatl*
Azteca
I am, I am

The precise calculation of time
in my Mayan mind

I hear the songs of Algeria,
of Africa
in my Moorish ears

I am,
I am . . .
rhythm
drums—timbales, congas, bongos
strike me with your hand
I sing tones your ears cannot hear

Strike me with a stick
my voice explodes horizontally

I am
electric guitar wailing La Llorona's
childless cries

I am
the desert, the mountains
& the contradiction is clear
as New Mexico sky

Tattooed to my existence
& shackled to my ankles

Watch me
hammer at the steel to make wings
Watch me
melt it to make blood

I take quartz from the ground
water from the river
smoke from the sky
& call my self American

I take the shame of Oñate
Navaho clay and the feathers
of Quetzalcoatl
& call my self *Xicano*

I take the pain of a bomb blast
the laughter from a playground
the blood of our ancestors
& call my self human

I am you
You are me
We see with taintless eyes
when we realize what we could be
& show the generations the forever
beyond their own skin

You don't know me, but
you think you do

You don't know me, but . . .
you do

You are me &
I am
you

You are me &
I am
you

You are (me)
&
I am
(you)

Daniel S. Solis

1995–2000

The golden age of Albuquerque Slam Poetry began as a time of rich and unpredictable possibilities. It was a time of ripening happenstance, a roiling pot of potential that would bubble over by 2005 and make 'Burque a Mecca not just for Slam, but for poetry in general. In early 1995 there had never been an Albuquerque Poetry Festival, Bob Swearingen had not published a book, Kenn Rodriguez had never slammed, the Taos Poetry Circus was roaring in the north, and Lisa Gill stood at the threshold of a flood of brilliant poems that would challenge and inspire a generation of fledgling 'Burque poets.

Juliette Torrez, high priestess of Albuquerque poetry, held court in the Dingo Bar, shaping sensibilities and the future of the city's poetry identity with her hosting, poems, and vision. Matthew John Conley proved both court jester and mage, providing comedic and passionate counterpoint with his piercing wit and raw and fearless poetry. Thrown into this volatile mix were poets like Traci Paris, Jim Stewart, Trinidad Sanchez Jr., Mitch Rayes, Socorro Romo, Henry (Enrique) Harrison, and an audience that was hungry for something fresh and real. The result was a scene that seemingly exploded out of nowhere into the consciousness of poets and hipsters across the country.

The four Albuquerque Poetry Festivals forever changed the face of the arts in Albuquerque and New Mexico. The 'Burque Poetry Festivals also fixed the city in the minds and hearts of touring poets from coast to coast. Besides being graced by numerous southwestern poets like Wammo, Mike Henry, Phil "Pony" West, and Genevieve Van Cleave, the festival featured Edwin Torrez from New York City, Daphne

Gottleib and Beth Lissick from the West Coast, and the one and only Shappy from Chicago.

The first Albuquerque Slam Team in 1995 consisting of Jim Stewart, Matthew John Conley, Trinidad Sanchez Jr., and Kenn Rodriguez did not make the semifinals at that year's NPS. Next year's team would make the semifinals but lose to eventual National Champs Providence by the narrowest of margins—on a time penalty.

It was a time when you felt like anything could happen, and often it did, from the emergence of Lisa Gill and Bob Swearingen as two of the state's finest poets to the arrival of poets like Eirean Bradley, Sabrina Hayeem-Ladani, Tamara Nicholl, MC Murph, Gary Mex Glazner, and Ken Hunt. It was a time of many and varied venues, from the Dingo Bar with its raw and chaotic ambience to the Sunday afternoon mellowness (usually) of Best Price Books and Coffee to Emma's Silvertone to the Gold Coast Coffeehouse, where the booze flowed as freely as the java and where people were once outside literally leaning through the windows of a packed house to listen to Beth Lissick's feature performance.

It was a time when raw talent met with singular opportunity and sheer good luck. It was a time of joy and risk and the insanity of something just being born, a time that will echo in the bones and the blood of every new generation of New Mexico poets who value performance as they value writing. ▪

Daniel S. Solis
No Part (a.k.a. Chicano Poem)

It is times like this
when I feel the old blood inside
stirring, heating
the new
Mexican
Mexicano
Chicano

I am listening to
Los Lobos.
Guitarron and accordion
spinning out generations
of dignified grief.
The soothing and sharpening of sorrow
by tequila's wet kiss.
The thrum-pop and cry of congas
Chepito talking bells
and the crack boom splash of *timbales*.
Santana's guitar wailing blue fire.
And I think about,
cutting off these long dreads
and slicking back whatever is left,
to look more like my folks want me to.
Like my uncle Joe,
the drunken barroom brawler.
Or like my father,
the sixty-hour-a-week man,
the union man,
the never miss a beat man,
the ladies' man on weekends,
much to the heartbreak and bitterness of my mother.
And something inside

Shifts
   Churns
      Slow
      moving
      like the juice inside the maguey

and I think of my uncle Jesse,
a huge man,
full of laughter,
bow-hunter
and the best dancer in the family.

And I think of my mother
as a young girl
raising her four younger brothers
following the crops from Michigan
to southern California
to Texas
and back again.

And I think of my grandmother,
bruja?
curandera?
Or both,
casting spells and prayers
by candlelight
pulling three-year-old me
out of near-lethal fever
that had baffled every doctor
at the hospital.

And I think of my grandfather,
at age fourteen,
in the coal mines of west Texas,
pitting fourteen-year-old

muscle and bone and tendon and pickaxe
against bowie knife and sledgehammer
wielding bullies and winning.

And a deeper thing takes hold
of what I am,
and being who I am,
there is no part of me,
that is not touched
stroked
burned
clutched—
by the heat and laughter
by the songs and tears
by all the lives of wildness and self-sacrifice
by all the lives of muscle and wisdom and
gamble
it took to come here,
here
the old blood and songs
mixing with
igniting the new
incandescent
unmistakably bladed and branded
simmered and shimmering
Mexican,
Mexicano,
Chicano.

Traci Paris
In Our 70s

If it's true
that we are given the lives that we
were promised and we live into our 80s.
And only then will we back right into our babyness.
Back to our walkers and strollers.
Finally back to our cradles,
swaddled and spoon-fed.
If it's true and we pull that slow reverse
that means the fire you and I walked through
in our teens,
we'll get to live in again
in our 70s.

In our 70s, you come over to my house
to get ready for the party.
We try on different outfits and
vie for the bathroom mirror.
We rediscover the secret that
the world can turn or stop
upon the shade of lipstick
we choose, in our 70s.

When we drive to the party
we listen to the pop radio station
and we know every new song by heart.
Because we listen to them night and day.
Because we know that these songs—
they were written for us in our 70s.

We slink into the party,
sneak into the bathroom,
take secret shots of tequila and
we don't share.

Then we go out to the backyard
(where the keg is)
and we smoke cigarettes and stare
at the big fat yellow moon.
Maybe we make eyes at the boys we don't know.
Maybe we kiss them behind the hedges,
hold their 70-year-old boy bodies tight against us.
And when they ask us for our phone numbers,
we just smile and wink.
We talk about those boys through seven intersections.
Like they were places we visited
on a road trip in our 70s.

We don't talk about "our day" like we might have
in our melancholy 60s, placid 50s,
mournful 40s, bitter 30s.
We know that today is our day in our 70s.
But our kids and our kids' kids
don't understand us.
They put us down,
say it's our hormones acting up again.
We just smack our gum and roll our eyes
and say, "you just don't understand
because you're not in your 70s."

You and me, Kid. You and me.
We'll slip out past curfew,
drive around, we'll be
the only ones awake in this dead town.
For the first time in fifty years,
that'll be us sitting in the back booths
of the diner, drinking black coffee straight.
I promise, once again
you and I will stay up all night,
talking about how
we're going to change the world. ■

Jim Stewart
Satellite Man

satellite man, satellite man
peekin' at your brain with an MRI scan
I turn on the microwave and crank it up to ten
to get you all hot for your satellite man

you were smoking in your underwear, sitting up in bed
when you felt someone knocking on the window to your head
from the sky at 60 gigahertz or more
you said, "let me get decent!" and I said, "what for?
'cause there's nothing really decent about what we're gonna do
and from where I'm sitting I can see right through
your little everyday world to your favorite show
and when you see my special offer, you won't say no"
so you picked up the remote, pointed at the set
tuned into my station and you started getting wet
then you took off all your clothes, called me on the phone
told me where you lived, and you said you're all alone
I said, "I'll be right over, don't make any plans
for the next couple nights, 'cause I'm a satellite man"

you went to radio shack to get your little girl a beeper
in designer pink or blue with pocket clip, so you could keep her
in touch, in reach, keep her up with the styles
and still buzz her anywhere within a thousand miles
and get her on the phone, hear her voice in your ear
tell her she's your baby, let her calm your fears
but don't you know if you can reach her anywhere, so can I
'cause you're on the ground, and I'm in the sky
more than 50 miles up, at 20,000 miles an hour
with a parallel set of RISC processors powered
by a 16-ounce plutonium core
guaranteed to keep me warm for a million years or more

I've got my little plastic finger in the pocket of her pants
and she won't take it out 'cause I'm a satellite man

now don't start crying about how it's not fair
you can't look me in the eyes and say I don't care
about your rights, 'cause no one's got a gun to your head
the button's in your hand, remember how you said
you can quit when you want, and use your own mind
the only thing I wonder is, where you're gonna find
someone else who will listen, who will be there all the time
to talk about your problems, and put it on prime time
coming up next
people who are jacking in just to have sex
for a real-time, real-world perfect simulation
with the smell and the feel and the taste of copulation
but it's quick and it's clean and it's absolutely safe
it's better 'cause you never look at anybody's face
the best part is, you don't have to lift a finger
it's an integrated, automated system; I'm the bringer
of light, of sound, of beta-wave bliss
saturday cartoons were never like this
you can try to turn it off, but I don't think you can
you've got me on the brain 'cause I'm a satellite man

satellite man, satellite man
sprayin' my stuff across the FM band
I'm on real late, so tune in when you can
and turn it up loud for your satellite man ▪

Amy Helms

December 1982

Member of the 1997 Albuquerque Slam Team.

My father bought his Harley-Davidson in
December 1982.
He wouldn't even let my mom
park her car in the garage anymore, after that.
She'd walk out to the curb
on those snowy, January mornings
and scrape six inches of frost from her windshield
with the heels of her navy blue pumps,
the same ones she'd trade her sneakers in for
on her lunch hour at work.
While her car was warming itself, sputtering back to life,
she'd glare at my father with this look—
a look that made me cringe
as I peered at her through the bathroom window—
the same kind of look she used on me
if I didn't put all of my Legos away
or I refused to eat my vegetables.
Those same cold, winter nights
I'd lay in bed with the covers pulled all the way over my head
and wait, listen for the accusations to start
once my father got home. He was late no matter what time it was,
and other sounds soon followed:
the sound of skin hitting skin, glasses breaking,
doors slamming shut.
I'd start to cry when the garage door creaked slowly open,
sounding like a faint, faraway cry for help,
and I could picture my father
pushing his bike down the driveway,
into the street, into the night
away from me, away from her,
waiting to start it until he was sure he was far enough away
he wouldn't wake me.

I'd muffle my tears against my Care Bear
when my mother came in to check on me,
a rum and coke held shakingly in one hand,
fresh blood dripped onto my pillowcase from a cut
on her hand or her head or her lip.
I couldn't blame him for hurting her, though.
It was her fault, she started it,
she always started it, and it was all I could do
to lay still, feign drowsy slumber
when what I really wanted to do was run after my father
and slap her pale, white cheek the way he had done
once
after a party when they came home late, drunk,
and thought I was sleeping soundly.
I wanted to tell her she had to leave him alone.
I'd give her my Barbie doll McDonald's,
the one Santa Claus had brought.
I'd go without candy for a whole year.
I'd eat broccoli without cheese
if she would just let him be
happy.
She wouldn't even go for rides with him.
No matter how much he pleaded she wouldn't go,
so he'd take me instead.
I'd wrap my arms tight around his waist,
feel safe
the way my mother felt safe
when she wrapped her long, tired fingers
around a half-empty bottle of vodka.
I snuck into the garage the next afternoon
while he was at work,
smelled the smells of oil and gasoline
I thought only belonged to him,
so I was surprised not the find him there:
sifting through buckets for a lost nail
or looking for a length of rope.

I was surprised not to see his Harley resting comfortably
under its brown, canvas cover.
I was surprised when my mother smugly told me
my father had sold his bike
so they could get that new refrigerator.
After that, my father,
he drank way more than my mother ever did.
He took my pictures off the new refrigerator,
told me I was leaving too many smudgy fingerprints.
He told me to play quietly in my room,
he told me he needed to be alone,
and I blamed her for breaking him.
I hated her for being so selfish she couldn't let him love
anyone, anything
more than he loved her and that included his daughter,
that included me.
I knew then
it wouldn't matter
if I ever learned to ride that pink Huffy
without the training wheels.
When I turned fifteen and went on my first date
it wouldn't matter
if the boy smoked or brought me home late.
My father would always be too busy to
come to my volleyball games, to help me learn fractions,
to care if I got an A on my French exam.
I would never be enough
to charm him back into the man he was in
December 1982
when he came home
with a bundle of silver, leather, brown polished metal
all made in the U. S. of A.
My father was a free man that day and for a little while
in the winter of my fifth year
he was whole. ■

Tamara Nicholl-Smith
Ash

I came here with twelve boxes on an Amtrak train
and holding a fist full of too late love letters
My car left a corpse in a Chicago parking lot
I barely noticed the hills or the blue sky
or the vastness of space between.

I came here to rid my self of myself
of the cash register ring of Kinko's copies
of the "Hey Honey" comments of cowboy hat wearin'
policemen, contractors and low end lawyers requesting "more fried okra please"
of the round and empty marble eyes of men who said "make it a double"
and "do you have a light?"
I always had one.
I watched the flame extinguish on the match, smoke rise and curl in circles around
cool desperate cigarettes,
I wanted to take the spent ash and press it to their foreheads
to call their souls back,
as if it were Ash Wednesday and I am asking them to give up their own death for Lent.

I wanted to run out into the streets of storm and clouds and shout
"save death for being dead"
run down Studemont past the bar doors,
past the grain silos, past the towers of smoke,
to the graveyard
where Stuart lay
with his crushed lungs
and arms like wings that took him soaring off the Corsicana cliff
into the unsuspecting valley
airlift to Tyler.

It took his lungs two months
To finally collapse under the weight of smoke and glass
Standing at the alter of his crushed lungs
Scattering rose petals to the wind
I whisper a promise
"I will save death for being dead."

The gray sky holds rain
and their eyes are gray marbles filled with smoke and rain
and their hands pass the time in three-hour poker games
while spit cups overflow with predigested tobacco.

We have taken a ride out to the West Side
where the volcanoes sit
distant protrusions
They sit quiet, surrounded by long dry grass moving in still waves.

This is where the earth spent its poison
threw its fist up in black boiling red raged anger and said
"get out of me that which does not serve me"
and threw liquid rock from its belly.

I am here,
with a handful of sky
and a promise to be alive. ■

Matthew John Conley

Slamming in the Early Years

Seeming cut off from the rest of the planet, nursing its own morbid sense of humor, Slam in Albuquerque in the late 1990s was an ORDEAL. Only held once a month, & only the top two making it to the second & final round, drama was constant & pouring like wet disco ball confetti on the heads of our booze-addled poems. We did anything & everything to amp the entertainment factor—awarding the biggest prize to first place, the second biggest to last place; Dead Poet Bouts between Kurt Cobain & Sylvia Plath, Haiku Dance Fever. We whipped poets & audience alike into a heightened state of Fitful & Ugly & Riot Laughter & we knew the whole world was listening . . . to the Duke City, that dirty phantom bus stop, repulsive & filled with the most stirring stories & pain. Poets lost minds they never had onstage at 313 Gold SW. Whether you were there or not, you can feel it in those late July thunderstorms. ▪

Figure 7. Second Albuquerque Slam Team, 1996. *Courtesy of Michael Hudock*

Matthew John Conley

Remembrance of Trinidad Sanchez Jr. (1943–2006)

Trinidad Sanchez Jr. was a member of Albuquerque's first
team at the 1995 National Poetry Slam. He passed away on
July 30, 2006, after suffering two strokes. His life and work left
an indelible mark on each of the communities he lived in and
he is best remembered for his passion in influencing aspiring,
young Latino writers.

> *We talked and talked*
> *and understood less.*
> *Stories of our ancestors,*
> *our history.*
> *We futurized*
> *of our death;*
> *how we would want it*
> *celebrated*
> *without being present.*
> *Music,*
> *whiskey,*
> *happiness,*
> *good memories . . .*
> *and no one cries.*
> —From "Death"

What I will always remember about Trinidad Sanchez Jr.
is his laugh, like a waterfall right when it breaks over the crest.
Trino always laughed louder & more often than anybody in
the room. His poetry was filled with joy, whether a meditation
on his father or a call for justice, & his warm spirit drew you
close no matter how grave the times. Though he was a few

decades older than me, I never felt a generation gap when we interacted; he was always right there, his eyes sparkling, his words stirring the unspoken truths inside of me. When he passed away on July 30, I felt a deep loss, not just for myself & the absence of a friend, but for the world we live in & the ears that yearn to hear even one moment of pure light. He was a great man, a great poet & *compadre*, but I carry his light & his laughter with me that I might live such a beautiful life. You will be missed, *vato*. ■

Trinidad Sanchez Jr.
Let Us Stop This Madness

The bullets from the guns
that massacred the invalids
in San Miguel, El Salvador,
the bullets from the guns
that killed the poet
in Johannesburg, South Afrika,
the bullets from the guns
that kill the actors on TV,
for no other reason
than our own enjoyment,
are the same bullets
from the same guns
that kill the children
in Detroit, Michigan.
The bullets from the guns
that killed Martin Luther King, Jr.,
that killed Mahatma Gandhi,
that killed Oscar Romero,
are the same bullets
from the same guns
that kill the children
in Detroit, Michigan.
When will it stop?
When will we learn
to listen to the artists
teaching the children
songs of life?
Let the children
grow into man/womanhood.
Let us stop weeping
for the invalids in San Miguel,
for the poet in Johannesburg,

for the children in Detroit.
Let us take a stand,
let us stop the bullets
from the guns
that kill our children.
Let us stop teaching
the children
that the bullets from the guns
are the only way
to deal with life.
Let us destroy the factories
that make the guns
that shoot the bullets
that kill our children.
Let us take a stand
to share life,
to break bread
with each other.
Let us stop this madness . . .
the bullets . . .
the guns! ■

Phil West

Remembrance of Ken Hunt (1970–2005)

July 2005

Ken Hunt died unexpectedly in a Chicago hospital in April 2005 due to complications from a seizure. Slam poets might best remember him as a member of the 1999 Albuquerque Slam Team, and he was also resplendent in drag as one of the scoreboard divas we dubbed Vanna Whites at the '98 Nationals in Austin.

But Slam poetry was only a sliver—albeit an important one—in Ken's life as a poet, musician, journalist, and a pure and sincere fan of his peer artists. Those who knew Ken witnessed both the fearlessness with which he wrote and the raw and jittery way he performed.

Ken and I created art together for years—first as poets and musicians in Seattle, where we met in the late 1980s, and later in the same capacities in Austin in the mid-1990s. Ken moved on to other cities and other artistic opportunities in his too-short life. He would later make homes in Madison, Albuquerque, Boston, and Chicago, but we discovered Slam together in Austin and were instantly drawn to the raised stakes and the energy implicit in its structure.

Despite his love of Slam and the poets who made Slam a vocation, Ken was never just a slammer. Though he battled through profound periods of depression, he was always able to find comfort and meaning and purpose in art and made deep impressions on many of the artists he collaborated with. Ken's work was consistently challenging, with artful allegories and confessional revelations laid bare on the same page. Happen upon his self-published books, and you'll find smart, passionate work that couldn't always be cradled within a three-minute time limit or an easy refrain.

Tony Brown has launched a new prize, commenced during NPS 2005, in honor of Ken. It rewards the best-written poem at an NPS, as voted on by competitors and volunteers. The Ken Hunt Prize is a fitting, and hopefully lasting, tribute to someone I was proud to call a friend, who always wrote as if his life depended on it, who wrote works offered up in the hope that they would matter and endure. ▪

Ken Hunt
Savanna

for everyone who has been tested for HIV

This blood which is being
drawn for the test is not
familiar blood: like watching
your closest friend go mad,
and you don't quite know
the exact nature of the change.
It is the vehicle
which has allowed me
to pass through all
these situations which have led
me to this clinic
where I give only my first name.
As the needle goes in
it makes a prick like every
laser light beam that hit
me square in the eyes
as I lived the accidental,
the ironic,
the physical life.

And these veins which yield
the sample are unfamiliar interstates,
the construction project
everyone forgot about,
prone to inducing the spill
of cargo. Careful, I tell
the clinician, I've been bruising
more easily lately
and I don't know why.
This is a bald-faced lie.
I want to say further, at night
I lie awake listening to the traffic

roar and gurgle inside me,
gridlock inside the skull.
Perhaps that is why all this
has come to pass:
to cut the noise,
decongest,
relax.

And the regimen to come,
I know it already:
Cut the misbehavior, stay
at home for a couple weeks
with herbal tea and the everyday
pressure of waiting. Eat healthy,
just in case, take vitamins,
and (you should have
done this already) stop smoking.
Concentrate on work and find
the Fox station which broadcasts
reruns of *The Simpsons*
three times a day.

And the voices, they will be there too,
figures from memory that do not
merit the dignity of being
called ghosts:
C'mon, Ken,
one more vodka and Coke,
one more shot of Jägermeister,
one more joint,
one more popper,
one more hit of X,
one more line of speed,
one more—

How many of us stumbled through high school
singing along with the Violent Femmes,
"Just One Kiss,"
and imagined it would come down to this?

As the needle is withdrawn
I rise above my body and watch it
unfold into a landscape
untouched by human works.
Savanna. Plains covered in tall,
reedy grasses. First the field mice come,
and then the grass snakes,
and then the gazelles and giraffes,
the wildebeests, and needless to say
the lions and tigers,
and finally the elephants.
Birds of prey circle, dive,
kamikaze contact with the earth.
I watch them progress in waves
until I realize it's an exodus,
that the fires have started,
and I am jarred back to my body to feel
hundreds of thousands of panicking
hooves and paws and wings
storming over every square inch of my skin.
I'm pinned down and suffocating. No
I bolt up in the clinic
chair to call out to anyone
I love enough to have hear me:
I refuse to become one of those friends
you will have to bury.

But the fact is,
my body is a landscape
and I don't know what lives there. ▪

Gary Mex Glazner
¿Por qué Lorca ha muerto?
For Federico García Lorca

As a child they bathed him in the red milk of the bull.
When he was a calf they turned his horns to the sky.

Young boy slept in a bed of hide.
Young bull fed the grain of bones.

Stands in the center of the ring, waiting for the children to sing:
today, today we drink the red milk of the man.

Horn and steel, the moment of forgiveness, the instant of prayers.
How sudden the hooves of the riderless horse!

The curious arrive each day. Desk empty of poems, waiting for the pen's return.
On the bed a shadow. You are full of children.

Can you hear them from the balcony?
Can you hear the voices coming to take you?

Smell the gunpowder? Sweet as assassins' eyes.
What will you teach them? How can they know you?

May we use the moles on your face to find the lost lemon of the moon?
How small these trees must have been when you were a child.

Did they shade you as you left forever? Did you ever leave?
The earth holds the molecules of everyone who ever lived, or ever will live.

Each breath we take is full of these uncountable lives.
The strum of your poems, the stomp of your deep song. *Olé*, forever *olé*!

He was the filament Edison forgot. He burned so bright the glass burst into a question.
¿Por qué Lorca ha muerto?

Tan Tan ¿Quién es? Soy Lorca I hear you are running in circles
asking why I am dead. Why don't you ask me? ¿Por qué no me lo preguntas a mi?

Now it is your turn. Take your time. Take time from the one-eyed moon.
Take time from ink that is closer to blood. Seek time from all the lovers

each moment they sweat with love. Place time in the deepest well.
Dip your cup into the green wet time. Let time fill your mouth. Let time fill your belly.

Siempre tiempo, Siempre tiempo. You are full with time.
Now is the moment to answer. *¿Por qué Lorca ha muerto?* ■

Lisa Gill
The Object

Perhaps the sun was coming up
and I was trying to douse it but
I dreamt I was filling light bulbs
with water to hold phosphorescent
fish. Artifacts displaced into
dream interpret differently. Or
perhaps I'm the one displaced,
the way the dove in my house,
looking for a perch, found, after
the ceiling fan turned, a 60-watt
in the track lighting. That sound
of birdfoot on bulb I didn't dream. ∎

Phil West

Albuquerque Poetry Festival

Tireless, driven, longtime host of the Puro Slam in San Antonio, Texas, where Slam poets go to cut their teeth, Phil West straddles page and Slam poetry. He is a local and national poetry organizer, flush with the success of his third Nationals in Austin.

> If the late 1990s marked an apex (if not the apex) for performance poetry in the United States, then the Albuquerque Poetry Festival was a major contributor. Though it was the energetic, often-rambunctious poets from Texas and the Southwest who dominated the festival lineups, poets from both coasts and Chicago with similar aesthetics converged on Albuquerque. There, they would find appreciative audiences and an atmosphere removed from the competitive mayhem, yet retaining the electricity of Slam. People came to the Festival not just to read and listen, but to be inspired, to recharge, to understand—viscerally if not cognitively—how powerful words on a page could be if spoken with the right degree of tenacity and conviction. ■

Phil West
The G-ification of Your Life

In the last few months, your life is more a palette of primary colors,
you find yourself naming things clearly and loudly, paying attention
to the way your mouth opens and closes and wraps itself around
sounds. You convinced yourself, when he was still in the womb, that
you'd give him a life free of television gamma rays, that it would
be nothing but books and wind instruments until the first day of
Montessori school.

This was before the cruel toddler wind blew through your house
daily, before you learned that at fourteen months, children are
fascinated with emptying things and filling things, but mostly with
emptying things. This was before you saw alchemy: what *Sesame
Street* can do to make your life easier for an hour.

This is chemistry: TV as a drug in its early addictive years. This
is your mother disapproving and you, teenage, protesting: it's so
wrong and yet it feels so right. This is you justifying: it's educational
television. This is you as American: a television you actually want
to hug.

He learned "yay" and unlearned it, he learned "God" and unlearned
it, he learned "mama" as a sign of affection that he uses before
he kisses Mom, Dad, Elmo doll, strangers. "Up" means pick me
up; "up" means put me down. "Bob" has stuck, however. Bob is
SpongeBob SquarePants, a talking yellow sponge. Bob is cartoon
fun for the whole family. Bob lines the walls of Target, is on a bath
sponge, is on Dad's underwear.

You're trying to connect the dots and call SpongeBob educational
television. He's learned to name Bob before he's learned to name
Mom, Dad, himself.

As a parent, you must navigate choices. Teletubbies, yes. Wiggles, no. You give the thumbs up to British people in pear-shaped costumes who seem to communicate by gurgling at each other in a prelingual dialect. You reject the saccharine Archies, staring at the DVD box, wondering if they are wig-wearing freaks, if those are really wigs. You are holding out. He responds to song and dance. Reality TV with performance: he is transfixed. Mouth open, rocking back and forth on one leg, clapping at the end of songs. He is connected.

You find yourself praising Scorsese for *Gangs of New York*—not for the artistry or the epic sweep, but for putting the bloody axe fight in the first five minutes of the movie so you can shut it off without getting too caught up in the film, putting it on your list of films to watch
after your toddler's bedtime, assuming he gets a bedtime that doesn't just happen to be the exact same bedtime as your bedtime. Thanks, Scorsese.

Three months ago, the family sat on the couch and watched *Scarface* together. Let Norman Rockwell paint that, yet it seemed what was on the screen was just a flutter of sound and light to your child. Now, you flinch at weapons across the screen, you ache to cover eyes and ears. You have crossed over. This is the G-ification of your life.

You wave a bitter farewell to Sunday nights with the Sopranos. Your child is a mimic, a sponge. You laugh, he filters. He is becoming. You are a slave to the sugar coating, the letter A, the number 3, the plush bodies of Muppets, a sponge living in a pineapple. You will reward yourself with animated movies that contain jokes for the parents. You will speak Pixar like your first love's name. Pixar. Pixar! ▪

Mike Henry
Forgetting to Live

We count out loud the things
that we have lost,
make them into books in rows,
into letters spelling names,
lists of names.

We are painted,
pale flesh or a carnival,
clowns or children
with dirty faces asleep
in new clothes, the near-smile
we are given will last awhile
and I am idle
I rest.

Say the words in any order,
nothing will change nor can
we stay a little longer
had I known,
would have decided I would
have said something
or fought
or stayed
or made amends
or did what I was told.

Reminiscence,
counting mistakes like marks
carved in jawbones.

Losing makes us stacks of bones
resembling men. ▪

Don McIver

2000–2005

Despite early roaring energy, poets can be a quixotic and rowdy bunch. It doesn't take much for things to fall apart, and it doesn't take long for a community to lose ground. By the late 1990s, ABQ poetry was in a kind of lull. The Dingo Bar had closed, and Poetry & Beer had moved to Sprockets. Sprockets, though a local bar, just wasn't a very good venue. It had the unenviable position of being in the space that had previously housed the much-loved Fat Chance, so people just didn't support it. Eric Bodwell and Danny Solis took the reins of hosting Poetry & Beer and moved it back downtown to Burt's Tiki Lounge (site of the former Dingo Bar).

In the fall of 1999, I started meeting with other poets: Amy Mullin, Sarah McKinstry-Brown, and Bob Reeves. The idea was to workshop our performance pieces in preparation for doing better in Slam. After Slam went mostly dark that fall, Amy and I jumped in unofficially to promote it. The finals that year were at Burt's Tiki Lounge, and the venue sucked. Unlike during the Dingo Bar days, the stage was pointed in the wrong direction, and you read to a wall with the audience on either side. I bombed, finishing dead last but vowing to figure this thing out.

We eventually lost the Tiki Lounge, Amy convened the first ever Slam Council, and we moved to Club Rhythm and Blues. Club RnB was a good venue, and the slam grew. Under the direction of the Slam Council, the disparate hosts—at that time only Kenn and Danny—actually communicated. The Grand Slam that year played to a packed house at then R. B. Winning's (now Winning Coffee Co.), and the team put out its first CD.

Slam was thriving again, and many new faces started appearing and slamming. In 2002, we moved the Grand Slam to the Outpost Performance Space and sold it out. Slam was on fire, and no matter what we did, it grew. By 2002, I finally cracked the slam team mystery and went to Nationals with another first-timer, Colleen Gorman—who was Diné and a member of the Angry Brown Poets, and the first Native American in Albuquerque to make a team—and veterans of 2000 and 2001 Manuel Gonzalez (a founding member of the Angry Brown Poets) and Carlos Contreras. We started doing school gigs with Write-Read-Succeed, making regular appearances on KUNM, and holding another monthly slam at the Blue Dragon, which I finally felt qualified to host.

Many new faces started to appear: Cuffee, Jazz Sena, Tony Santiago, and Damien Flores. Hakim Bellamy found my e-mail on a website and asked how he could get involved. I told him, "Come to slam. I'm hard to miss." He did, winning the first slam he'd ever been a part of and making the 2005 team. The rest is a convergence of history and circumstance. ■

Figure 8. Don McIver at Hotel Blue during NPS 2005. *Courtesy of David Huang*

Don McIver
Mo Ainm

Missoula, Montana.
    Garden city of Montana.
"Many Rivers" converge in the valley that is the city.
My muddy past is resurrected in slides.

I, a short round faced boy, a *brogach*,
    towheaded and shy,
    visited the home of *mo seanair*.

My grandfather, this white-haired, decrepit, old man grabbed me with
    hands, *lamhan*, made of the stone that he mined,
    hands, *lamhan*, like the rocky soil that he tilled,
    hands, *lamhan*, made of the skins of those potatoes
    he planted, watered, dug up, and ate.

For years I would spend summers with him,
leaving my sisters, my mother, my father, my friends,
to be with this tired old man, smoking Camels.

This tired old Scotsman,
    he clung to me with those potato-skinned hands,
        divied out dollars because I was his blood,
            I carried his name, *ainm*.

Without consciously trying,
    he made me proud of this name.
McIver, son of Iver, *ogha Iomhair*.

Now I write to connect;
    his past buried in mine,
        his blood buried in mine,
            his name buried in mine, *mo ainm*.

Missoula Montana.
Many Rivers Montana.
Many days of my winding youth converge here. ▪

Colleen Gorman
Jesus Was a Mutt

Jesus was a mutt
Half Deity, Half Skin
Skinny,
knobby kneed
and darker than the shades allowed by King James's Book.

Like the rest of us,
he sprung forth from the womb-belly of the Earth.
Hands spread open like stars,
he reminds me that the divinity within us
also comes from the Star People.

His story repeats itself infinitely.
Mother Earth manifests herself as Changing Woman.
She enchants the Sun with her shifting skin and naked petals.
Dressed in beads of water,
her scent preoccupies him with lust,
and her chocolate chip hills entice him to taste her sweetness.

Dancing droplets of light
transform His presence into prisms on Earth.
Our imperfect minds can only see His shadow,
the rainbow.

In essence, the Creator descends with passion to rain
furies of kisses upon her body
and run rivulets of fingers through her hair.

Reincarnation reflects itself in the many faces of Junior.
Buddha is reborn again as a praying mantis
who happens to pray
at the same time
every day.

Like Jesus, children of the Sun and Earth are deities
with hearts composed
of the Sun's blinding white heat and
the sea salt of birthing waters.

Horizon's blue line twinkles shooting stars
as Father Sky pulls his blanket close.
In exquisite joy, he closes his eyes,
squeezes his warm Sun heart down and
imagines to life babies
babies,
babies bursting from Mother's round brown belly.

He imagines to life babies!

We are all children of the Sun and Earth.
Indigenous Peoples!
Those of us who understand this World and Universe
as living entities.

And like the rest of us,
Jesus was a mutt.
Half Deity, Half Skin
Skinny,
knobby kneed
and darker than the shades allowed by King James's Book. ▪

Amy Mullin
Zarathustra

"[O]ne must still have chaos in oneself to be able to give birth to a dancing star."
—*Nietzsche*

When I come down the mountain,
I will be immense:
my flesh will radiate desert nightfall
and I will clothe myself in quasars,
wear the sun in my cheeks and eyes,
and take the moon as a lover
meteoric progeny assailing the skies,
the cosmos perspiring.
constellations will seep
into my braincase
rearrange synapses in their design,
my mind will birth galaxies in a blink.

My heart will be bright and hot
as a nova exploding
without fading away,
and my spirit will soar,
kissing each planet and cooing its secret name,
bathing my laughter in the tails of comets.
ordinary gods will use
the architecture of my radiance
to score the music of the spheres,
and even the stars will sing.

Zarathustra,
I will cradle your loneliness and love
in my immense hands,
sweep the dust from your soul with my breath
arrange my arms and legs in new patterns

to pay you homage with the skies' pictures,
I will thrust you from the black hole eclipsing your heart,
spin you backwards on the ecliptic until
you are a child in the heavens,
climbing the firmament
like a rock wall,
rubbing your palms
against blistered asteroids—
pain and joy
expressed with stammmmmmmers.

When I come down the mountain
to be the universe itself,
you can sleep the
peaceful slumber of the
child under my sky,
knowing that
your prophecy
came true. ▪

Bob Reeves
Quincy

(A neighbor girl pointing to an
old tomcat in the sun & telling
L. W. "That's Quincy. He don't
care about nothin'.")

I'm Quincy.
My eyes aren't even as open as they look.
I got a second pair of eyelids if I want the world mellower, I got this tail I can twitch
when anything improper comes along like some nuisance factor in my sun, like tardy
milk, like wind & rain.
I've heard the opinion this stuff is Acts of God.
I'm Quincy.
God & me pay no attention to each other.
I got that car I can get under:
what's He got?
I clean myself with spit,
God tries to clean the parking lot with rain.
My method actually works. Why can't He cut it out?
Leave the sun where it is, it's just fine.
I'm Quincy. I'm just fine.
Your lover screwed you over, you'll never love another?
You're too over-the-hill to get the job you could really get into?
You got a drug problem, life don't make much sense without that needle, that bottle,
that cable TV, that hand job, those stars & stripes wavin' on the mast of that destroyer?
Ask me if I care.
You probably care, or you know you oughtta.
You care about universal health coverage.
You care about the Bosnians.*
You care about love, salvation, next month's rent, findin' beauty in a wasted world,
findin' life in death.
I dunno, maybe you care about me. You care about yourself.
You care about the rain forest & bringin' down your intake of saturated fat.
Go ahead.
I'm Quincy.
I don't care about nothin'.

*[insert your current favorite victimized people]

Manuel Gonzalez
Alburquerque

With watermelon mountains
melting misconceptions
with marijuana dreams and contemplative confessions
Cholos chasing *chicas*
living *Mi Vida Loca*
like the ancient *Mexica*
with kicked backed khakis
that camouflage clown faces
We smile now but cry later
break-dancing B-Boys battling the cross fader
My name is Alburquerque but my friends call me
'Burque

Mi Madre makes *masa* with Flour and *Manteca*
Rolling out her Tortillas
and Scraping Spices in the *Molcajete*
just like the ancient *Azteca*
as *Tolteca* knowledge is passed down from the ancestors
and *mi madre* lights a candle for *La Virgen de Guadalupe*
My name is Alburquerque
but my friends call me
'Burque

As the sands of the *Santuario*
silently call the sound for my soul
and the Patience and Perseverance of the *penitentes*
plant the seeds that will one day make me whole
the Legions of Mary who pray the rosary
for humanity
who don't have time to bend their own knees
My name is Alburquerque
but my friends call me
'Burque

Politicians like balloons
both floating on hot air
while I stare at the sunset
seeing Reds,
Oranges,
Pinks,
Purples,
Blues
and that Blue/Black color of the magic hour
where the mystical existence of spirits is evident
for those with eyes to see
My name is Alburquerque
but my friends call me
'Burque

Listening to Saturday morning Traditions
played by Musicians
the founding fathers of my self-image
hearing *Rancheras* and *Cumbias*
and those *Boleros* sung with a teardrop on the vocal cords
Y Volver
Volver
Volver
My name is Alburquerque
but my friends call me
'Burque

I was named after a Duke
who never left Spain
and being Junior without ever knowing your father
brings a lot of pain
My name is Alburquerque
but my friends call me 'Burque

Don McIver

Venues—Winning Coffee Co.

There's a different art show up today. This one is from a high school, while last week the art hanging on the walls of Winning Coffee Co. was from ArtStreet, an open studio that is part of Healthcare for the Homeless. To say that Winning is just a coffee shop is to miss the point entirely. Located less than a block south of Central on the "Harvard Mall," Winning Coffee Co. is one of the hubs of the Albuquerque art community, or, at least, where the art community gets their coffee. Need to connect with an old friend who's not answering their e-mail? Just start going to Winning's, and eventually you'll run into them. Want to swing dance, pick up a copy of a small local poetry magazine, find out what's playing at the local black box theaters, or read at a poetry slam? Then you don't have to go anywhere else. The bulletin board is cluttered with announcements. Their bathrooms are both co-ed even though they are clearly marked Male and Female, respectively. And once a month, MAS Poetry Slam and Open Mic, hosted by Kenn Rodriguez, kicks off in the main room. MAS Poetry is the second-oldest slam in ABQ, but the first all-ages slam, which during the slow dark months of winter still kicks as poets read to the people who are trying to escape the cold, peer in from the street, and bum cigarettes from the people on the patio. ■

Esther Griego
Road Trip

Thoughtful and calm under pressure, Esther Griego was a member of
Albuquerque's 2000 Slam Team and coached the 1998 and 2004 teams.
She was the lead designer of the 2005 NPS program—no small task.

This road will not remember us,
this highway
midnight strip of gravel and tar
tattooed across dusty landscape
of shrub-spotted, cactus spiked
hills, turning one over another will not
recall the spinning of our tires
past gas stations, mailboxes, and mile markers.
It does not treasure the overpasses, rest stops, and
speed traps it carries us through.
This road does not care that I read to you, hum
along to the
skip of a CD, that
our fingers mingle, sticky, together,
or that I love you.

I run
laps around your silence
sift through your scars to shake out
stories, like war torn
banners from a deserted adolescence.
We drag our fingertips
across the faces of mountains,
count license plates,
colors of cars,
and watch for eighteen-wheelers
slumbering on shoulders and off-ramps
like beached whales.

This road does not care that we are tired,
eyelids flutter and snap open to the
slashing light of oncoming traffic
our muscles ache and
atrophy, motionless, strapped to this
aluminum cocoon of movement, we hurtle,
faster than the darkness, waiting for the
next town to surface, sparkling, until
the road pulls at it with the impatience of a
single breath, the fleeting memory of one more
restless mile,
dragging it,
abruptly
beneath the horizon. ■

Joanne Dominique Dwyer
The Hour of the Angelus

A Santa Fe poet, Joanne Dominique Dwyer was an original member of the 1999 Albuquerque Poetry Slam Team before the grueling practice schedule and commute took its toll. She was Taos Poetry Circus Grand Slam Champion in 2000 and is now an MA candidate in creative writing at College of Santa Fe.

I am tired from the imagining—
the thought of a woman's breast, instead of a man's.
The Angelus bells that ring inside my mind.
In French class the Mademoiselle
said my name was Jeanette,
but she didn't tell me Jeanne d'Arc
was sentenced to death
for wearing the clothes of a man.
The Mademoiselle didn't tell me
what her own crime was—
but I could see the punishment
worn on her skinny white arm:
the inked numbers of a vile tattoo.
At the inquisition the bishops asked
Jeanne d'Arc how she knew that
the voice she heard
was that of the Archangel Michael,
she replied, *"Why He spoke in the tongue of an angel."*
To imagine is to conjure color,
to sense the outline of a winged body.
To love is to lie down with Lady Death—
a descent is a falling into birth.
What would you do with a child who heard voices, saw visions?

The Mademoiselle had white hair,
while mine was still the down of a child's.
I learned to say
Je suis fatigue and *Je t'aime.*

I wish I could have said to her
Je suis désolée—
I am sorry.
I wish a voice would have said to Jeanne d'Arc
Put on a dress if it means your life.
Someone saw a white dove
fly out from the fire that burned Jeanne's body.
And the executioner, later interviewed
said he could not get her heart
to burn into ash,
so he threw the heart of Jeanne d'Arc
into the river Seine.
And now France can claim the highest
per capita rate of Prozac consumption.
And I am tired from the imagining—
The wearing of men's clothes was to protect her among men
for the Devil cannot exert his power over a virgin.
I am tired from the imagining—
the constant urge to re-break the seal of my virginity,
to peel the duct tape off my nipples,
walk into the center of town bare-chested,
wearing the pants of my grandfather.

If Jeanne d'Arc were alive today
would anyone believe her
if she said she heard the voices
of St. Margaret and St. Catherine in the wood?
Or would she be court-ordered
into the office of a psychotherapist,
given a script for Symbyax,
coerced into wearing an Yves Saint Laurent dress?
Would anyone believe me
if I said it is the hour of the Angelus,
the tolling of bells?

White dove having escaped the fire
with a sprig of Jeanne d'Arc's hair in your beak—
every downstroke of your wings
is felt in our lungs—
every descent to the deep,
every drink of water,
every woman wearing pants
carrying the heavy weight of armor. ◼

Dale Harris

Central Avenue

Poet, publisher, editor, supporter of all things poetry in Albuquerque, Dale Harris organizes an annual poetry variety show in April at the Harwood Art Center and hosts an open mic every month at Winning Coffee Co.

Central Avenue and its predecessor *Willow Street* came out of informal backyard get-togethers at Cathryn McCracken's Albuquerque North Valley home in the summer and autumn of 1999. A number of talented writers gathered, including Bob Swearingen, Lisa Gill, Sarah McKinstry-Brown, and Mitch Rayes, grooving on each others' poems and later submitting work to the new publication. Bob Reeves took over the editing of *Willow Street* from December 2000 through October 2001. *Central Avenue*'s advent was in December 2002. Shortly afterward, I assumed the lead editing role with Bob Reeves acting as "midwife" doing copy layout, and Cathryn McCracken as a contributing editor.

Willow Street established a pattern of community building that continues with *Central Avenue*. Monthly issues are released at regular open mic poetry readings in the University of New Mexico area. The first Thursday *Central Avenue* readings are currently held at Winning Coffee Co., and the mood there is lighthearted and very receptive to first time readers. The books are chapbook style, simple, attractive, and affordably priced. The original cover, an imaginative scene of *lobos* on a park bench under a streetlamp, was designed by Kaia McCracken. In 2006, Adam Rubinstein created several new, eye-catching covers for *Central Avenue* and began printing its monthly issue runs. In its first four years, *Central Avenue* published well over a thousand poems, the work of 175 differ-ent poets from throughout the Southwest. *Central Avenue* is entirely supported by sales of issues at readings, yearly sub-scriptions, and occasional unsolicited small donations. ▪

Dale Harris
Manzano Sunflowers

You missed Indian Market and of course, the sunflowers.
As usual they swept across August,
at first a few, a yellow trickle along the fence line;
then more, making pools in the pasture
and splashing down into the *arroyo*;
then incredibly many more,
dappling the distance as though
a giant hand had buttered the land.

Yet with the entire prairie to expand into
they prefer crowds of themselves.
They mass along the roadsides lined up
as though a parade were about to pass.
Here and there one stands alone but not for long.
Soon his kin will come and there will be
sunflower squalor, a floral slum.

Once out they will not be ignored.
Stretching their skinny stalks, they top our roofline,
press against the window screens, peep in at the door.
Familiar footpaths to the outbuildings are obscured
and from the road we seem afloat,
our cabin an odd tin boat in a sea of sunflower faces.

They are the most staccato of flowers.
I catch them humming snatches of polkas
and John Philip Sousa marches,
bobbing in the breeze to the Boogaloo,
the Boogie-woogie and the Lindy Hop.
I call their names, Clem, Clarissa, Sara Jane
to try and tame them.

My neighbor comes by, she has a field full.
They're useless, she complains;
her horses won't eat them.
I should hope not, I exclaim after she's gone.

I don't remember if you even liked sunflowers
but you liked life and they are all about that.
Today I wrote to your family finally.
I expect they are occupying themselves
with beautiful gestures
in order to get over the grief of you.
As for me, I have sunflowers. ■

Cathryn McCracken
Treelove

grandfather elm
keeps me on a sweet tether
a roll and swell
lengthening me

leaves like hands which power
and come
I am larger than life
voice like an animal

the men are gone
to please their separate selves
they never guess what I have found
what makes me swell

I am a ragged piece of light
when they return
warm from dancing
his sap covers my arms and legs
inside me seeds, gendered
by the cross

I only smile
no one asks
I never tell

when the baby comes
she will have a green heart
and eyes that are full of sticks and leaves. ■

Sarah McKinstry-Brown

the rag

Figure 9. Sarah McKinstry-Brown
and Daughter at NPS 2005.
Courtesy of David Huang

Late 1999, Lisa Gill, founder and editor of *the rag* and its monthly sister reading series Herland, called to ask if I would take over as editor and coordinator. Because it was Lisa on the other end of the line, I was immediately reeled in, eager to take on something I'd never done before. A women's-only reading series and zine had created healthy debate within the wider poetry community, and the need for such a reading and publication was clear: Herland was one of the best attended reading series I'd seen, and the women who gathered monthly at the Harwood weren't just there to read, but to listen, debate, volunteer their ideas, time, and resources towards *the rag* and Herland. Just as heartening was the packed audience at Herland's quarterly public readings where Herlanders shared their work with the public at large. Herland's numerous anthologies, appearances on KUNM, and sponsorship of touring women readers created a more diverse and inclusive poetry community. Virginia Woolf asserted that for a woman to be able to write she needs a room of her own. Lisa Gill's vision went beyond that, growing a room of her own into a community of our own. ▪

Sarah McKinstry-Brown
After the Ultrasound, Week 12

You should know your big sister is prone to stomping
small things. Not yet two
inches long, you're safe—
for now. Still, before your first breath,
I'd like to say I'm sorry for yelling,

for forgetting to pick you up
from school, for the Coca-Cola Slurpee
you can't have, for FM radio,
split atoms, American cheese
and the ozone
hanging over you like a sieve.

Sorry for the 5, 6 and 10 o'clock news,
and for fattening you up with Disney.
I'm sorry for 13, Yellow #5 and mandatory
Pep Rallies. I'm sorry for your first French kiss
for laugh tracks, Improvised
Explosive Devices and Standard
Aptitude Tests.

Sorry for footnotes, specifically, *Ulysses*,
for Depleted Uranium, Sunday nights
and "Eleanor Rigby" playing on Musak,
in Applebee's.

Someday you will come across
pictures of this ultrasound and of Saturn's rings.
I'd hoped more of this world
would be left
to your imagining.

Don McIver

Venues—Club Rhythm & Blues

Nob Hill is prime real estate—clearly the coolest part of town, but not necessarily the best place to open a live music club. For a few short years, the owners gave it a try, at first booking Blues exclusively and then adding anything that drew a crowd. Thus, when Poetry & Beer left Burt's Tiki Lounge, moving up to Nob Hill on a Sunday night was a grand idea. The room was wider than long, with tablecloths and candlelit tables creating just the right ambience that suggested sophistication and art/performance appreciation.

On one Sunday a month, people packed in for poetry: Poetry & Beer specifically. Club Rhythm & Blues was clearly the classiest joint to slam in. It had a certain caché, a certain charm, and out-of-town poets graced its stage, drank too much, and entertained.

But, alas, the venue wasn't meant to last. In the fall in 2003, the bar started showing signs of financial distress. Advertisements disappeared from the local newspapers; the staff shrunk in size; and finally, just a month after Poetry & Beer moved to the Golden West, Club Rhythm & Blues closed, thus ending poetry's first foray into a bar in Nob Hill. ∎

Jerry Mondragon

A Vato Needs All the Help He Can Get

Full to overflowing with norteño suave, *Jerry Mondragon first went out for the Albuquerque Slam Team in 2003 and made it onto te team in 2007. Jerry's creativity also takes form through acting, writing and touring plays, and painting* retablos.

Sunday afternoon, *el sol afuera*
Y rucas galore showing just enough to make your, you know what,
stand up and take notice
Pero en mi ranfla mas suave, I become the focus of their attention
Wraparound dark shaded sunglasses hide my staring eyes
Don't wanna let them know I'm taking the first look

I stretch my elongated neck to take a quick glance at my *linda cara*
on the rearview mirror
Reassured, *me despacio*
Giving *las* baby dolls more precious time to observe
The *vato* behind the wheel

Mi carucha, is my pimp
A two-ton aphrodisiac with slick lines
supported by a set of chrome plated *chanclas*
that'll slow dance its way to the . . . promise land
Guaranteed, *no te miento*
Pero what can I say
A *vato* needs all the help he can get

And just like that
Se me acaba el recuerdo y me pega el pinche reality
Trapped in the remnants of a past long gone
Time shredded to a fraction of a past long gone

Now I'm a potbellied, hair losing, burp gulping, *pedo* shooting *vato*
cruising down the same road in my 1986, fifty mile a gallon, Yugo

Que chinga when the most pleasure you get is from a much needed piss
Your old lady's idea of sex is a three dollar ninety five cent pint of Häagen-Dazs
And your quality of life has totally betrayed your expectations

Deep dreaming darkness shadows my fast dimming life
I've lost my *huevos* that used to crank up my *ganas*
and with each passing day, it seems much harder to wake up
I wish I still had my shiny *ranfla*
'Cause a *vato* needs all the help he can get ■

Tony Santiago

Venues—Insomnia

Three-time City champion, Tony Santiago was a member of Albuquerque Slam teams in 2003, 2004, and 2007 and the 2005 Santa Fe Slam Team. He is the proud father of Samantha.

A coffeehouse is a sad, dead thing devoid of personality until the people show up and inject life into it. Such was Insomnia, a place I went to in late 1999 when a sign caught my eye.

"Open Mic Poetry Show Begins This Wednesday with Your Host—the Outsider." I had acted onstage and done stand-up onstage, but never in all my years had I heard of poetry being read out loud to an audience. My friend dared me to give it a shot, and so . . . I did. But, on the first night of the show, our host, the Outsider, never showed up in favor of attending an Alphaville concert in Denver. Much to my chagrin, Insomia's owners told me the show was canceled unless I wanted to host it. I didn't really want to; however, I knew if I didn't go up to read that night I never would. Knowing nothing of how poetry shows were run, I decided to host in the comedy/variety show tradition, and the owners seemed happy.

The next week, the Outsider returned and hosted the show on and off for eighteen months with me serving as his backup host the whole time. Insomnia became a safe haven for ABQ's Goth community and gay community as well as the often-stoned community. It quickly stood out as the poetry show for those a little bored by poetry shows. Every Wednesday night, poets, comedians, rappers, and faux vampires would test their newest material on an audience craving something a little raucous, politically incorrect, and high energy. The Outsider left the show, asking me to take the ball and run, saying that "this far-too-serious town needed it." But, and he made this clear, I was to read a piece in between every poet called up. I naively accepted and began writing seven to twenty new poems a week in the hopes of keeping the show fresh. (Two or three of those were almost good!) This continued until about April of 2003 when Insomnia closed due to the fact that aside from Wednesday nights, when attendance was higher than any other poetry show in town, Insomnia remained virtually empty the rest of the time.

The management warned me two years in advance that this might happen someday, and I threw a monthly Poetry Slam into the already-crowded four-shows-a-month schedule. This actually hurt attendance more than anything else. Insomnia was and always had been a show for the people who couldn't give two shits about the scores.

When Insomnia closed, I was devastated. Where would we all go? For me the answer came three days later when I won the first of five city championships for myself, a triumph I believe the good people at Insomnia trained me for. The encouragement I received from the patrons was a godsend.

After all, a coffeehouse is a sad, dead thing devoid of any personality until the people show up and inject life into it. ▪

Tony Santiago
Ode to Johnny Cash

Listening to "Delia's Gone" on a Saturday made me realize a few things.

If Johnny Cash were a sandwich,
forget about it.
He'd be a hoagie, you know?
With extra meat.

And if Johnny Cash were a woman,
he wouldn't insist you buy him some stupid dinner.
He'd be fine, and he'd put out just for the fuck of it!

If he were a ride,
he'd be a roller coaster, too,
the kind that makes you vomitacious,
with big loopty loops and crying children.

And what if old J. C. turned into a robot?
Let me tell you right now, MONSTER'S BEWARE,
'cause that rockin' son of a bitch
would form Voltron,
the Lion One too.

As a planet, he'd be Jupiter.
As a superpower, he'd be flight.

And if Johnny were a motorcycle,
he wouldn't be one of your little
Honda, Suzuki, Ninja
pieces of homoerotic shit.
He'd be a big old hog, Harley or Chopper, baby.

If you ain't heard the glorious baritone majesty of the Man in Black,
well boy, you oughta.
Not only does he have the same initials
and blood alcohol level of our Lord and Savior,
but if he were a party,

he'd be the kind at the end of an '80s movie,
stunk, drunk and full of punks,
with rock 'n' roll blaring while whores of every color
swing from chandeliers.

He's a whiskey flask filled to the brim with poetry.

He's a lion with the taste of blood.

He's a wallet chain with spikes taken directly from Jesus's crown of thorns.

He's a rebel.

He wouldn't wipe his ass with the American flag.
He'd wipe it with the shroud of Turin,
then write a song about it.

If the Cash man were a car,
he'd be the batmobile.

If he were a soda,
he'd be Jolt.

If he were a love song,
he wouldn't be one of yer
Celine Dion, Hollywood strokin' ballads of Loserville.
He'd be "Delia's gone, one more round, Delia's gone."

You see, as a child his mother told him if he became a policeman,
he'd wind up captain.
If he became a priest, he'd wind up the pope.

Instead, he became a songwriter
and wound up as Johnny Cash. ▩

Bill Nevins

Committing Poetry in Times of War

Local poet and former Rio Rancho High School teacher Bill Nevins watched as the assault on civil liberties caused by the run-up to the war disbanded the school slam team. For encouraging students to write about their opinions on the Iraq war, he was fired. The fight that ensued and the support he received put Albuquerque in the spotlight for poetry on the edge.

Spring 2003: U.S. bombs fell on Iraq. Rio Rancho High's Military Liaison hearing "disrespectful speech" (student poetry critical of No Child Left Behind) over the PA system demanded the responsible party be "horsewhipped."

Poetry Slam team coach Bill Nevins was fired, his team shut down. The principal had a student poem read, warning peace protestors to "shut your faces."

Students called the media. Nevins sued. Rallies supporting the student poets happened in New Mexico, New York, New England, and even New Orleans.

The school paid two hundred grand to settle, but Nevins stayed fired, and the student poetry team stayed shut down. There's a movie out about it all: *Committing Poetry in Times of War.* ■

Don McIver

Venues—Blue Dragon

Just a month after it opened, the Blue Dragon started host-ing poetry events in the summer of '99. The owner, Bill, a shy poet, wanted to create a space where people could hang out and listen to live music, songwriter circles, poetry readings, and open mics. Initially he was open to anything, but when I approached him about doing a reading, he, psyched by the turnout, offered a monthly slot and then didn't book any poetry events other than the occasional one-off readings so as to not compete with mine. Don McIver & Friends, and then the Blue Dragon Slam, was the only poetry reading at the Blue Dragon, but in 2006 a second slam was started, and the Blue Dragon became home to two slams per month. The Blue Dragon slams boasted big audiences that came because they knew when they would happen as opposed to finding them on a flyer (what flyer?). Kids hung out, ducked outside for illicit cigarettes, and ducked inside for poetry. Occasionally, the counter help would wind its way through the crowd look-ing for a plastic figurine to exchange for the organic pizza they're carrying. Through three different owners, the Blue Dragon remained loyal to the poetry nights, never once trying to change the deal: a meal for the feature/host and twenty-five dollars cash in prize money. ■

ABQ Slams

City Champions and Slam Teams 1995–2005

ABQ Slam City Champions

1995	Trinidad Sanchez Jr.
1996	Jim Stewart
1997	Daniel S. Solis
1998	Kenn Rodriguez
1999	Daniel S. Solis
2000	Tamara Nicholl-Smith
2001	Sina Sao
2002	Kate Makkai
2003	Tony Santiago
2004	Tony Santiago
2005	Hakim Bellamy
2006	Cuffee
2007	Jasmine Sena Cuffee

ABQ Slam Teams

2006	2005
Hakim Bellamy	Hakim Bellamy, City Champion
Jessica Lopez	Carlos Contreras
Lee Francis	Cuffee
Damien Flores	Esmé Vaandrager
Kenn Rodriguez, Co-coach	Kenn Rodriguez, Coach/Member
Esmé Vaandrager, Co-coach	

2004	2003
Tony Santiago, City Champion	Tony Santiago, City Champion
Cuffee	Jerry Mondragon
Esmé Vaandrager	Kenn Rodriguez
Don McIver	Daniel S. Solis
Jasmine Sena Cuffee	Don McIver, Coach
Libby Kelly	Eric Bodwell, Manager
Damien Flores, Alternate	
Kenn Rodriguez, Coach	
Esther Griego, Asst. Coach	
Angela Williams, Asst. Coach/Manager	

2002	2001
Kate Makkai, City Champion	Sina Sao, City Champion
Manuel Gonzalez	Carlos Contreras
Don McIver	Mike 360
Carlos Contreras	Kenn Rodriguez
Colleen Gorman	Sarah McKinstry-Brown, Alternate
Daniel S. Solis, Coach	Daniel S. Solis, Coach
Kenn Rodriguez, Alternate/Asst. Coach	Eric Bodwell, Manager

2000	1999
Tamara Nicholl-Smith, City Champion	Daniel S. Solis, City Champion
Esther Griego	Tamara Nicholl-Smith
Manuel Gonzalez	Gary Mex Glazner
Aaron Trumm (a.k.a. MC Murph)	Ken Hunt
Andrea Guest, Alternate	Joanne Dominique Dwyer, Alternate
Eric Bodwell, Coach	Eric Bodwell, Coach
Kenn Rodriguez, Coach	

1998	1997
Kenn Rodriguez, City Champion	Daniel S. Solis, City Champion
Matthew John Conley	Amy Helms
Eirean Bradley	Matthew John Conley
Daniel S. Solis	Kenn Rodriguez
Sabrina Hayeem Ladani, Alternate	Jim Stewart, Alternate
Esther Griego, Coach	Traci Paris, Coach

1996	1995
Jim Stewart, City Champion	Trinidad Sanchez Jr., City Champion
Matthew John Conley	Matthew John Conley
Kenn Rodriguez	Jim Stewart
Robert Wilson	Robert Wilson
Traci Paris, Alternate/Coach	Kenn Rodriguez, Alternate

Chapter Four

ABQ Poetry Brings NPS Home— the Organizers' Story

The National Poetry Slam began in San Francisco in 1990. Since then the event has traveled to Chicago, Austin, and Seattle, among other cities. In part, NPS is dictated by the national organization Poetry Slam, Inc. (PSi). There are certain requirements for the number and type of venues, depending on the number of teams registered to compete. There are certain expectations for favorite daytime events and Slam family traditions. But each city brings its own personality to bear on the event as well. And so, each year at the SlamMasters' meeting, representatives of Slam communities from around the country make their best pitch with their best perks to win this challenge, this honor: to organize and host the National Poetry Slam.

SlamMasters represent registered venues from across the country that host a regular poetry slam. Anywhere from sixty to seventy-five of these local poobahs gather each April in the city that will be hosting nationals the following August to visit and critique the preparations for the upcoming NPS and discuss other Slam community business. They also hear bids for the NPS two years out. The discussion that ensues on the bids can be by turns hilarious and harrowing, and the outcome will either commit the bidding group to a foreseeable future of the most grueling (and rewarding) organizing, or send them home with a lost opportunity to provide this service to the Slam family and their community. ■

Susan McAllister

The Bid

Director of the Harwood Art Center, Susan McAllister was a financier and organizer of NPS 2005. She is an ardent supporter of poetry in general and Slam poetry in particular (and supersecret, private poet herself—don't tell her we told you!).

Weather: It was cold when we arrived in Chicago in April, National Poetry Month, for the annual PSi SlamMasters' meeting. We had anticipated the cold, but it did bring home the point that winter lasts much longer in Chicago, in a lot of places, than it does in Albuquerque. Weather was a big selling point in the bid. Sure, New Orleans is great, but in August? Think of the humidity! Albuquerque's hot, but at least it's a dry heat.

Heavy Lifting: The meeting was upstairs at the Hideout in Chicago. It was as cold inside as out. The stairway was narrow and dim. We lugged a lot of stuff up that stairway: boxes of salsa shipped from Albuquerque, which arrived intact, mostly; boxes of multicolored, hand-decorated gift bags with "I Love Albuquerque" buttons pinned to the handles and handmade clay chiles suspended from ribbons with *www.abqslams.org* printed on the back tucked inside. We lugged boxes of bound-paper bids, fifty pages each, explaining why Poetry Slam, Inc. and the assembled SlamMasters should select Albuquerque as the city in which to hold their annual convention, the National Poetry Slam. We proved we could do the heavy lifting.

Funds: The SlamMasters' meeting was long, really long, and the bids were on the agenda for AFTER lunch. We were glad of that. Better to ask people to trust you with their big event when they are full and happy. Marc Smith approached us as the SlamMasters were breaking for lunch. He slipped forty dollars into my hand and suggested we run around the corner to get some sodas and water. Good sign: he trusted us, almost total strangers, with money. Later that afternoon, we presented one of the most detailed and complete budgets ever submitted in a bid.

Vision: A lot of people think of Albuquerque as a small town, sometimes even those of us who live here and love this crazy city. But Danny had a big vision for NPS 2005, and we put together a bid that did that vision justice. The presentation we made to SlamMasters raised the bar for all prospective NPS hosts; it was detailed, professional, ambitious, and smart. It also had poetry.

> *With the Rio Grande pumping life through the*
> *heart of Aztlan*
> *pumping breath in the words of storytellers*
> *pumping passion in the hearts of warriors*
> *flowing freely like the tears of mothers*
> *My name is Alburquerque but my friends call me 'Burque*
>
> *Listening to Saturday morning Traditions*
> *played by Musicians*
> *the founding fathers of my self image*
> *hearing rancheras and cumbias*
> *and those Boleros sung with a teardrop on the vocal cords*
> *Y Volver*
> *Volver*
> *Volver a tus abrazos otra vez*
> *My name is Alburquerque but my friends call me 'Burque*

Manuel Gonzalez—"Alburquerque"
excerpt from 2003 version

It's easy to come up with a hundred reasons not to do something. We knew the SlamMasters could imagine double that number of reasons NOT to hold the Nationals in Albuquerque, and they did. From hantavirus to a decided lack of mass transit, from not enough potential audience to "who doesn't want to go to New Orleans?"—we heard it all. But all they needed was one reason to say yes. And Albuquerque, the underdog with the jeweled collar and no tags, gave them that reason. We promised them the best National Poetry Slam ever, and they believed us. ■

Figure 10. NPS 2005 Sticker. *Courtesy of Kenn Rodriguez*

Susan McAllister
Front Porch

We walk three steps up onto deeply shaded, wraparound, screened where
the tall, thin, Irish boy
holds my hand sweetly
all night long and only one kiss
as if I were delicate as seedlings in May,
fragile as pressed flowers.

Clematis twine around aluminum posts and small shingle roof,
a physics major
walks me home after three margaritas and a shot of tequila to boot,
passionately explains the Theory of Relativity
as if I were white-hot brilliance
blown out from nothing, rapidly expanding.

On a Brooklyn stoop, six stairs to windows watching, small pot of geraniums,
a gentle man, still dark, with silver
in twilight shows a photo of two girls, nieces,
wishing for things to be right for his own
as if I were green valley fertile,
arms open to welcome sun, or rain.

Sit awhile on this porch with me
Share the view from here

I won't ask you in; that would be too close. ◼

Daniel S. Solis

The Vision—a Bigger Boat

When I came to the Albuquerque Poetry Festival from Asheville in 1996, there was an amazing amount of poetry in and around the city. As I watched the festivals unfold over the next few years, I began to realize how much Albuquerque loved the art of spoken word and to understand the incredible potential that poetry, performed, had as a force in the community. I watched as scantily advertised readings turned into standing-room-only literary "happenings." These performances generated money for the venues that hosted them and wonderful performance opportunities for the poets involved, but most importantly these events generated an opportunity for people to get together and experience something they couldn't get anywhere else. The raw vibrancy of these shows was heady and addicting. You could pay little or nothing and see a show unlike anything else around, something profound and profane, hilarious and heartbreaking.

Despite the uniqueness and power of this fledgling artistic movement, many seemed to undervalue the poetry and the poets themselves, as though this "poetry thing" were some sort of mildly amusing sideshow, some peripheral flash in the proverbial pan to the honored mainstays of the artistic community—music, theater, dance, and cinema.

For the next ten years I and others in the community would fight this condescending and ill-informed attitude toward performance poetry and its practitioners. (Indeed, the fight continues today.) Progress was slow and incremental, so much so that some poets and organizers discouraged the idea of even bidding for a National Poetry Slam in Albuquerque. Some felt that the city wasn't big enough to support the weight of the largest poetry event in the world. I thought of National Poetry Slams I had attended where audiences for preliminary bouts consisted of 25 or 30 people in a room that could hold 150.

But having watched and helped the 'Burque poetry scene grow over the years, I realized that audiences needed no convincing. Albuquerque had (and has!) an abundance of art lovers who respond with enthusiastic appetite to any performance poetry sustenance set before them. I truly felt the community was ripe and waiting for an artistic event on the scale of NPS.

It was sometime in early to mid 2003 when Susan McAllister and I first talked about potential audiences for an NPS in 'Burque. We broke it down to preliminaries, semifinals, finals, and daytime events. We figured that on preliminary nights—Wednesday and Thursday—75 to 100 people per venue would be an excellent turnout. With eight venues in play simultaneously on those nights, that would put our total audience between 600 on the low end and 800–1,000 on the high end. We figured that prelims would generate buzz for semis, and that would mean 200 to 300 people at each of the four venues, meaning our numbers would grow 800 low end to 1,200 high end. We felt that if everything went perfectly, by the time Saturday night finals rolled around, we could sell about 1,000 to 1,500 or more tickets to the finals at the Kiva Auditorium. The Kiva seats about 2,300, so add the 500 or so poets and coaches and posses, about 100 comps and the above-mentioned sales, and you have not a sellout, but a decent house for your big night.

As far as daytime events, we were hoping for 200 to 400 general audience per day on top of the poets themselves. Throw in another couple hundred for after-hours events, and our estimated total audience was about 4,000 to 6,000. This was an unscientific eyeballing of the figures based on our city's population, the size of the venues, and various other factors both logical and superstitious. We felt the estimates were realistic and respectable.

Then something strange began to happen. Everywhere I went in the city people would mention the approaching National Poetry Slam. People would ask me about it—the dates, the ticket prices, what cities would be attending, what venues were involved. We were still almost a year out, and the NPS buzz hummed around the town like some sort of low-decibel mantra woven into the periphery of the everyday.

I knew we had been doing a good job of getting the word out, that Don McIver was an excellent media wrangler, and that the event itself was more than worthy of healthy attention and turnout, but I was still unprepared for the sharp and growing interest that greeted me at the coffee shop, the grocery store, bars, theaters, and newsstands. I couldn't even walk to the mailbox in the morning without someone prancing up to me with an inquisitive look or hanging out of the window of a passing car to shout requests for NPS information.

I went to NPS organizational meetings wondering if everyone there was as spooked as I was, but everyone there seemed to be fine, blissfully unaware of the growing storm we seemed to be sitting on. Unaware of the increasingly obvious reality that what we thought was a good-sized marlin was actually the daddy of the shark that made an hors d'oeuvres out of Robert Shaw.

I sat in meetings having visions of huge crowds outside packed venues, angry and out of control with poetry lust, waving their festival passes, which would get them into NOTHING because all the venues were full. I saw the city in flames. I saw the organizing crew being put under arrest by the city fire marshal for overcrowding venues. I saw myself slowly being lowered into a vat of bubbling liquefied laminates by a maniacal crowd of Slam fans chanting "BLAME SO-LIS! BLAME SO-LIS!" The sirens of the approaching riot squads would provide the funerary wail of our crumbling NPS attempt, and all the while a great fish would be circling in the murky Rio Grande, chuckling, waiting for a tar-covered and defeated poetry organizer to wade out into the current to wash away the shame and the hurt.

"We need a bigger boat!" I blurted out.

Everyone looked at me as though I had just announced that I was on acid in the middle of church. They tried to ignore me and continue with an orderly meeting.

"No, really," I said.

It would be months before anyone was really convinced of my vision. I felt like John the Baptist raving in the desert.

I knew we had to be ready. I envisioned wonderful capacity crowds at every venue—happy NPS goers having the time of their lives, seeing all the great poetry that time and fire codes would allow. I saw poets from all over ecstatic about performing for standing-room-only houses. I saw a Saturday night sellout at the 2,300-seat Kiva Auditorium. I diligently kept in mind that one of our biggest responsibilities was to the poets who had worked so hard, sometimes for years, to win a spot on a team, hoping to make it to semifinals and dreaming of gracing the Saturday night finals stage in a beautiful, packed theater. I knew all of these things could be a reality if I could only convince my colleagues of my premonition about the coming crowds.

If I could not convince them, we would end up in the dark place, the bad place.

Now when I would blurt out, "We need a bigger boat!," everyone would laugh and I would laugh with them—the mirth of the happily unaware and the village madman.

Eventually almost everyone was badgered into belief by my unceasing harping on the possibilities of bigger-than-expected crowds.

The rough numbers for 2005 attendance eventually came in around 18,000 to 22,000 for the four days of 'Burque's NPS, easily three times the "high end" number of 6,000 we estimated two years out. We were ready, with enough volunteers and organizational work. We adjusted on the fly to various trying circumstances and unforeseen roadblocks, skillfully navigating potential fiascos with the dexterity and nerve of a Mississippi riverboat captain and crew. (I feel like bellowing out "Mark Twain!" right here.)

At the finals on Saturday night, the "Spirit of the Slam" trophy was still at the trophy shop, which was closed. Susan McAllister ran out frantically and purchased a piñata as a stand-in trophy. It was a piñata in the shape of a fishing trawler, a boat, and it was exactly the right size. ▪

Figure 11. Eric Bodwell Delivering the Stand-in "Spirit of the Slam" Trophy. *Courtesy of David Huang*

Daniel S. Solis
Fat Man

SEE THE FAT MAN! FAT ALBERT!

THE FATTEST HUMAN ON EARTH!

walking down the midway with Vicki
to the clank roll and thunder
of the giant ride machinery
hidden behind stretched
once bright
now fading
canvas
lights lock bars
cheap speakers blaring
cheap pop hits
coupons asphalt
and lines for rides like
the Himalayan, wild mouse
black widow, caterpillar
tilt-a-whirl, bubble bounce
presided over
by road weathered men
tattooed slack
with boredom
cigarettes dangling
from indifferent lips
and Vicki says,
"Let's go to the freak show!"
we go to the one where
for a certain number of coupons
you get to view
a variety of freaks
more freaks per dollar
what a bargain

I have forgotten most
of what I saw
in that shadowy tent
that day
there was a black man called Popeye
who could make his eyes bulge
way out of their sockets
a couple of listless pygmy goats
and Fat Albert,
not black like the cartoon Fat Albert,
surprisingly not eating,
just sitting watching TV
the barker led the crowd
from freak to freak to freak
giving the spiel
and each one did their
little freak dance
then it was Albert's turn
the barker talked about
how many pounds of bacon
and dozens of eggs and biscuits
Fat Albert had for breakfast
then Albert gobbled Twinkies
for the crowd
then pushed the play button
on a cheap cassette deck
Little Richard tinny howling
"AW Rudy! Tutti Frutti!"
and Albert began to swing
his enormous gut
from side to side
bulbous fat filled pendulum pushing
open his shirt's bottom button exposing
a fish white triangle of skin
and as the crowd laughed
I looked into the eyes

of this man
this Fat Albert
and saw something less than hollow
like negative space
his mind was somewhere else
dreaming of not even god knows what

Slim beautiful women?
a sun filled road he walked
as a child?
porterhouse rare, salad
and stuffed baked potato?
a *Gilligan's Island* rerun?
the cool hands of his
mother on his forehead

and he caught me looking
and flashed silent anger
"Get out my eyes you sonofabitch!"
and I did

then Vicki and I
tumbled back out onto
the blue skied
autumn streaked midway
and we talked stealing—
that is "liberating" the pygmy goats
to a hippie farm but that's another story
and later that night
playing percussion with a reggae funk band
pounding the congas
guzzling Guinness Stout
drumming harder than usual
drinking faster than usual
I could not drink or drum
Fat Albert's eyes

or the crowd laughter
out of my head
could not shake the thought
that I was a part
of a so-called civilization
that lived off
and laughed at
and sucked on loneliness
and I played so hard
my fingers split open
like they hadn't in years
and I wrapped my swollen digits
around a fresh one
icy cold
drained it
in two pulls
on my way
to the dressing room
where I burst in
grabbed our drummer David
by his jacket
pulled him toward me and said
"Look man! If I go crazy and start smashing shit,
and they come and take me away,
tell everybody
it wasn't the Guinness; it wasn't the Guinness!
It was the Fat Man!"

Laura E. J. Moran

Behind the Curtain

Grand Slam champion in Providence in 1992 and Seattle in 1996, Laura E. J. Moran was an NPS 2000 organizer in Providence and appears in Albuquerque when the performance poetry folks need anything, including help with Carol Boss's KUNM Women's Focus *radio show to advertise for NPS 2005.*

September 2000: Nationals over. Bills paid. Sponsors happy. Poets returning to all corners. The Providence 2000 Nationals organizers stare into blank walls—no last-minute ads, no bags to fill, no housing complaints, no emergency e-mails, no tracking lost volunteers, no malfunctioning microphones, and no more protests. All in all, in retrospect, we did alright. Nobody was arrested.

We tried new things. Some worked, some didn't. In the end, all of us wanted to be at least an arm's length from Slam and the Nationals—at least for a little while. A little while for me turned into five years. No Nationals for five years.

April 2005: I open my e-mail to find a note from Danny Solis and the Nationals Committee with an invitation to run a couple of workshops at the ABQ Nationals. To be frank, the Slam world turns so quickly, I had thought 2000 ancient history—let alone the eight years before of teams and touring. With the advent of Def Poetry Jam and Bullhorn Collective and the many ways our community has grown, literally tentacling out through time and space . . . well . . . who'd remember me?

Turns out many people—and that is what I love most about Nationals—reunions. Thousands of miles, many years and still the hall-running hugs, the cross balcony hoots, the

4:00 a.m. breakfasts, and now the new children, the new poets, the new friends.

Reminiscing aside—I saw changes, like a time traveler, a little distance clarified my perspective. The ABQ 2005 committee was so organized. Administratively smooth and capable. Venues were gorgeous. Their community wholeheartedly behind the huge commitment as was evidenced from the start at the Opening Ceremonies and even before that within the welcoming arms of Hotel Blue.

Putting on Nationals means more than juggling logistics and equipment and protests. It means years of advance work priming the locals, generating cultural interest, assessing your resources and the resources of the nearby communities. It means reaching out to undiscovered potential for poetry lurking in your hometown, exemplifying commitment, artistry, aesthetics, and excitement. The welcome in ABQ 2005 permeated the streets. The locals knew the poets were coming and why they were visiting and were palpably invigorated about the events to happen. The ABQ 2005 committee and hundreds of volunteers created that magic carpet that all the poets flew for the four days of the festival.

AND SO MANY POETS! To carry that many teams requires a sound, functioning infrastructure—the man behind the curtain, if you will, has got to have his head on straight. As the days progressed, the virtuosity of the planning grew hand in hand with the virtuosity of the visiting poets. Day events concentrated at the National Hispanic Cultural Center helped to keep everyone nearby and accessible to the events. Matthew John Conley's exquisite "hai-coup" victory proved that it's not all about finals night, and the exuberant audience at the group piece event proved the audience loves the art form as much as the competition.

It seems the organizers took a good, hard look at all the past Nationals, sussed out what worked, what didn't, took the good, tossed the bad, created lasting changes that filled in the holes, carried themselves with grace and tenacity through the sticky spots, and above all tried to respect the fledgling poets, the vets, their local community, and the audience. If I had to sum up my experience at ABQ 2005, the word would be smoooooth. One other: CONGRATULATIONS! ▪

Laura E. J. Moran
Misfits

Then there was Montgomery Clift
bronco spill after spill
his battered whiskey skull

unraveling Marilyn's lap: her kind thighs,
indian pony eyes, canyon cleavage.
Her lassoed wild brain slapped down to her ass.

Oh—to rub America's quivers the wrong way,
to the last black and white,
to the damned end

swallowing dirt,
abandoned rust,
the hangover of an unforgiving sun.

To the teeth I say—
to the gift horse and stupid
truth, a bit in her mouth. ▪

Don McIver

The Media—Getting Albuquerque Excited

We started publicizing the event a year ahead. Strategic advertising and word of mouth made up our media plan. Kickoff events helped build the necessary hype. One was a fund-raiser at the city's KiMo Theatre, featuring former Boston City Champion and two-time competitor in the Taos Poetry Circus, Patricia Smith, with several key Albuquerque poets, including former Albuquerque City Slam Champion Sina Sao. We also reprised the Poets' Diner to raise funds and awareness in April in conjunction with National Poetry Month. Almost thirty people bought tickets for a meal at Graze, ordering their favorite poems from a menu, which were served up by circulating poet minstrels.

Past that, the plan was to focus on getting the news that NPS 2005 was coming to people who would actually attend— people who already attend live events, read local papers, and listen to community radio. Many people think you should target national press and television to get an audience to an event this size. Frankly, I don't agree. Not only did I not care that *NPR*, the *New York Times*, *60 Minutes*, the local television news, etc., weren't responding to my e-mails, I didn't think they were important. Local television stations finally paid attention to the event after covering opening ceremonies. The story was so compelling and the energy so palpable that they gave us news coverage for the rest of the week. By then, the event was well on its way to being a success without their help.

KUNM (college/public radio): Because I had established a relationship with the station as a volunteer, I enlisted KUNM as a sponsor even before we got the bid, and it ended up sponsoring us big time. First KUNM donated over one hundred public service announcements (PSAs), which we used to promote events throughout the year but saved most (seven to fourteen per week) for the two months before NPS '05. One repeating ad aimed to build anticipation, purring that "It's almost here." The station also agreed to broadcast National Indy semifinals (safe harbor after 10:00 p.m.) and part of finals (after 10:00 p.m.), which meant even more PSAs to announce the special broadcasts. I ran that through PSi—an easy sell. Numerous people have commented about hearing it on radio and the internet. As the event got closer, I cultivated relationships with DJs and got poets on as many different shows as possible. The week of Nationals, I had poets on afternoon shows Monday through Thursday. Everybody loved it.

The Alibi (local weekly paper): *The Alibi* at the time was the trendier of two art weeklies. Since Nationals, the other one has folded and a new one has started, but the *Alibi* was the one I pushed. I'd been getting press hits from it for years, and since I knew and wrote for the Art/Literature editor, I knew he would help me out a lot. He did, giving us mentions in almost every listing of poetry up to the event. For example, "The 2005 team does a fund-raiser to help get them to NPS, which will be in ABQ. . . ." My first hit was when we were awarded the bid. The week of the event, we got the cover story. We also negotiated cheaper ad rates, and our ads ran starting in April, with fewer in May and June, ramping up again in July.

The *Albuquerque Journal* and *Tribune* (a.m. and p.m. daily papers, respectively): I had a relationship with some of the writers and knew they would give us something. I followed up with them about a month before the event to see if they needed/wanted anything. When Taylor Mali came to town for a separate function, I set up an interview for the *Tribune*. I ended up buying some ads in the *Journal*, too.

New Mexico Daily Lobo (University of New Mexico student daily newspaper): UNM's student newspaper did a cover article in its welcome back issue. Of course, it helped that UNM had a slam team and that the Art/Entertainment editor used to work for me in a previous incarnation as a restaurant manager.

Corporate Radio: I drive a lot, so I listened to a range of radio stations for potential targets. The radio stations all want you to buy across their groups, which I did not do. If the station was album-oriented rock, pop, hip hop, or alternative, I was interested. I didn't care about ratings, because I felt a specific type of person would be interested in Slam. Thus, I avoided the top-rated rock station and all the top-rated country stations. I wrote the scripts for the ads and tailored them for what I perceived as their audience. The commercial for the alternative station was akin to a wrestling commercial, while the album-oriented rock station big in Santa Fe featured a softer voice conveying the same information over some jazz piano. The ads were timed to play ten days before finals with about six to seven spots per day per station. In all, we advertised on five different stations.

Grassroots (Internet, flyers/posters at local hangouts): Our approach locally was to plaster as much of the city with NPS as we could reach, sometimes quite literally. We printed bumper stickers, postcards, posters, and flyers. I found as many on-line calendars as possible and listed there very early. A local collaborative blog, Duke City Fix, agreed to offer daily coverage during the event. At every poetry function for months before Nationals, we enlisted the help of local poets to pass out flyers and hang posters in three parts of town most likely to bring in audience members: downtown, the Nob Hill–University area, and the North Valley. We hung posters in multiple bookshops, checking them regularly to see if they were still up, and re-hanging as necessary.

One time, in the process of handing out fliers in Nob Hill, I actually went into a shop and left my journal and PDA behind. I freaked. I'd just gotten the PDA from work and dreaded telling my boss I lost it, so I waited and waited. One day I get a call from Gary Mex Glazner saying somebody called him looking for Tony Santiago and if I had his number. Of course I had Tony's number. Gary explained that Tony had left his journal and something behind at a store in Nob Hill. I said, "I think that's mine." I called the place and discovered that they called Gary because his number was in the book, and Tony's name was the only one in the book, and yes, the "something" was my PDA, battery worn out but still functioning.

I guess publicizing NPS made me a little scatterbrained, but the result of all our grassroots efforts to build excitement and word-of-mouth anticipation was packed venues for almost every event. This wild plan that ignored much common media wisdom brought people from all corners of the city—people who bought festival passes so they could come back to multiple events. The targeted grassroots approach slowly built the buzz that crescendoed during the festival, as each event created bigger and better waves, turning out people that we never dreamed we could reach. ■

Patricia Smith

The Magic of Performing in New Mexico

Some of my most energizing, controversial, rewarding, and frustrating experiences as a poet have had the sunwashed environs of New Mexico as backdrop. On the stage of one of the Southwest's most elegant theatres, almost blinded by the stage light, I've felt love come back from the darkness. I've stood at the front of classrooms and been reminded how exhilarating the exchange of creative passions can be. I've even joined the circus in Taos and turned my love of words into pure recreation. Even then, I had a sense of being in an exquisite space, a place where I could revel in the possibilities of my art. There's a kind of magic in New Mexico. It's a haven for any writer, a place where there are no limits, where you can be absolutely what you're meant to be. ■

Figure 12. Event Flyer for Patricia Smith.
Courtesy of Esther Griego

Patricia Smith
Waiting for a Title in German

Bitterfeld, Leipzig, Landsberg. On the staticky
radio, an American Negro is marching to Zion.
Neely screeches *sheep!* as the wool blitzes by.
Luis is at the wheel, all gritted molars,
sweaty palms and musical Mexican expletives.
None of us dares look at the speedometer,
but with the window rolled halfway down,
we spit gnats from the surface of our teeth.
The Autobahn has refused to know us,
won't ease roar and wind to fold us in,
so we chatter Our Fathers and notice,
for the third time, that the seat belts are busted.
If we hit anything, we die, Luis observes—
no concussions, no slivers of glass in the eye,
no slow-motion rollovers. At this speed,
we would be extinguished, our bodies
would be red mist and smoke. We wonder aloud
at our own obituaries, shamed by the tiny blips
we'd leave behind—notebooks of indecipherable
stanzas, self-published tomes, blurry VHS tapes
of ourselves reading to ourselves.
Fighting for a clear signal on the one station
we sometimes understand, we cheer as Sam Cooke
twists his plaintive tenor to beg Jesus for several favors.
We'll just get in line behind him.
Dominique, drunk on warm wine, hefts an empty,
belches fragrantly,
asks if that's Austria we just passed. ▪

Don McIver

Venues—Puccini's Golden West

God only knows how long Puccini's Golden West has been open. The place is definitely old, struggling to prevail through the whims of ABQ development and desires, becoming sometimes the coolest place in town, sometimes a dive. But in the fall of 2003, knowing the National Poetry Slam was coming to Albuquerque in the summer of 2005, Poetry & Beer called the Golden West home. Though a cool bar, it was not an ideal fit for poetry.

First, the place was too big. And long. The stage sat at one end with the other end hosting the beer taps and a pool table. People always wanted to crowd at the far end of the bar, near the beer taps, even as we moved the tables closer to the stage to try and make the room more intimate. With a monthly reading, filling the Golden West became a monumental task, but one we tackled because we knew we wanted to use it as one of the venues for NPS. In most of the other readings, if we brought in fifty people, the place seemed full, intimate, cozy, but at the Golden West if we didn't bring in at least a hundred, it felt empty. Second, in order to make the room cozier we'd have to get there early and rearrange the furniture. And third, having survived downtown for years, the management only accommodated us so much. While we had some success at the Golden West, including sold-out bouts during the 2004 Southwest Shootout, some spectacular shows for traveling poets, and three nights of bouts during Nationals, we moved Poetry & Beer once again after Nationals. Although we were still on good terms, the Golden West was just too hard as a regular venue, so we moved to a smaller venue with plans of staging bigger shows at the Golden West in the future. ∎

Maresa Irene Thompson

Organizing NPS 2005

Poet and organizing force behind NPS 2005, Maresa Irene Thompson champions women in the Slam scene and has found her rightful place onstage as a host of the Firestorm Women's Poetry Series.

I equate the experience of producing NPS 2005 with that of Extreme Childbirth: a thirty-three-month gestation period followed by four days of chaotic birth, adolescence, middle-age, and retirement.

The actual four days of the event are still a blur tangled by fragmented memories and a haze of emotions: anxiety, exhilaration, panic, joy, resentment, bliss, exasperation, gratefulness, exhaustion, relief, and love.

Bound together by our dedication and commitment to the event, the members of the NPS Organizing Committee met weekly for eighteen months. Being part of the group was one of the most memorable and enduring parts of NPS due to the deep friendships that evolved. It was also the most harrowing and trying part of the process. Frequently, we strongly disagreed over the organizational details. None of us had ever organized an event of this magnitude. We had no road map to follow and were all winging it.

Producing NPS 2005 was my personal gift to the community. All of the hard work and physical and mental sacrifices culminated in a special place and time where the world came together in verse. I have never felt more proud to be from Albuquerque, New Mexico, than during finals night as I watched the Albuquerque team win on the stage we prepared.

Would I go back and do it again?

Yes (but differently). ▨

Figure 13. Daniel S. Solis, Maresa Thompson, Esther Griego, and Susan McAllister at NPS 2005. *Courtesy of David Huang*

Maresa Irene Thompson
Renaissance Women

Me and Lori
sitting under the kitchen table at that high school party
watched feet stumble to get another drink
snowflakes of pot shake on linoleum

these cardinal sins of indulgence could not satisfy us more
than a bag of potato chips a bowl of M&M's
and real non–Diet Coke

it had to be underneath the table
on that dirty kitchen floor
that we could share our secret obsession and true love
Calories and Fat

At home our mothers with their
Health-conscious, exercise-frenzy, NutraSweet-inducing,
Fat-free, and low-cal diet of a lifetime
would have gawked
at this indulgence

Like the time we had a fry tasting contest
of all nine major fast food restaurants
(Wendy's won with Long John Silvers a close second)

and went home to leaf through magazines
where the remotest likeness of our curves could not be found
so we turned to art books and found
Real Women, Big Women
with Round Bellies and Full Hips

We knew that we were born in the wrong time
had we been born during the Renaissance
we would have been the models
posing nude upon velvet couches
for our images to be immortalized in oil

Yet one single trip to the mall
told us that size 0 exists
and we're living in the wrong time
So we get cookies and milkshakes
and Lori turns to me and says:
"Show me a woman with abs of steel and I'll show you a traitor."

Suck it in

You're sucking it in
she's sucking it in
and I'm sucking it in

holding back those rolls of fat
suppressing our very belly buttons

every day women suck it in
to fit into clothes that are too small

I remember being ten years old
and learning from my mother that
women suck it in

I would practice and concentrate so hard
that eventually it became habit
now I suck it in
in my sleep

I bet if we could get those
security video tapes of dressing rooms
we could see every single woman
sucking it in
as she tries on New Clothes that don't fit

What exactly would watching all those video tapes tell us?

Millions of women aren't breathing.

Girl Scout Cookies

What we need is a revolution
a second renaissance

Gather your *Vogue*s, *Elle*s and *Mademoiselle*s
gather your Celebrity Workout Videos
bring out your Healthy Choice ice cream, Slim Fast, Dexatrim and
SnackWells Cookies

we'll pile them all on the mountain
and burn them as we
dance naked and eat Doritos.

A revolution like that would take a miracle
so I'm going to hide in a box
of Girl Scout Cookies
made for girls
made by girls
to support girls
to comfort girls
Thin Mints could never make me fat

And I tell myself that
one day
the revolution will come
it will stop
I will stop
hating my body

One day
I'll stop
sucking it in ■

Adam Rubinstein

NPS Experience

Founder and creative energy behind Destructible Heart Press, innovative designer and surreal page poet extraordinaire, Adam Rubinstein moved to Albuquerque months before NPS to help and stayed.

Moving here sight unseen before NPS assured that the meetings would sound like a sloshing mix of English and the hum-whine of a vacuum cleaner. I didn't mind; I was sure they were saying something useful. I opted to work on the program 'cause that was graphic, and we could all understand pictures. Esther and I burned half of June and July studying programs, reading typography books, hammering down our master-piece. Soon I realized it was her project, and I jumped ship.

When things got rolling, I moved downtown. I knew enough of the city, and I wanted to be on the frontline for my poets, 'cause I hadn't really *done* anything yet. I venue managed at the Launchpad in five consecutive bouts. Not recommended. Like so many, I fell prostrate before the Lowrider of Limitless Beer. Caught sight of a lot of naked poets. Definitely recommended. And I worked backstage on finals night, so I saw it all, and couldn't hear one damn poem.

Whole thing burned me out for a good six months, but finally, I'd done something for my community. Sort of. ■

Adam Rubinstein
Courting the Spark

Sometimes the city breathes heavy
down my shirt, the lofts and bars
and office buildings and their loyal suits
and the streets full up with sunshine
and tacky shoes, the women with Yesterday
wrapped around their hips
like the hand of a man who stares back too hard,
the supermarkets unflinching and bereft of tomatoes,
the neighbors' dogs howling their sad and dangerous music,
the *vatos* who make downtown a fun house of grease
and belligerent compliments,
the pickups and their rednecks
who drive down my tailbone revving
like their balls were tied & throbbing
to the gas pedal,
the rich houses by the golf course
out watering the lawn at noon with their mechanical families,
the mile upon mile upon
upon mile of sprawl
that is the city's arms afraid
and ashamed of its heart
or its face,
the businessmen who rise dirty
every morning to unwrite the dance of the dead,
and we are no cleaner than them
and we elect them to glove our hands
in movers' boxes,
the traffic lights that know
precisely when you are approaching,

and the wind that crashes
me into you, cheap hello, cheaper
how are you, full of good-bye & get out of me,
the bars over our windows like snakes' teeth,
the freeways full of dead frogs
croaking their way home,
each standing on another to see where the holdup is,
sometimes the city does this, too,
and bottles her hate
from an exhale
and finds me
in Lowe's on Lomas
in the afternoon
and frowns at me, silly *gabacho*
and holds her shoulders like a falling statue
to my anger,

and I think,
Maybe it's time to move.
Maybe I am a walkway obstruction
in a sea of walkway obstructions
yearning to swing over Albuquerque
on her countless telephone lines
become the current that travels my voice
to California—
I want to weather the summer of travel,
open my eyes under a different street sign
every five to seven days
and kiss the nape of a city
that will love me hard
as 'Burque
with after-hours bars between her teeth
and an infection
that means we can't play tonight.

C'mon, Albuquerque, bring me back
the stale orange slice of Orlando
the fog & promise & thundering karaoke of Portland
the drunk smirk of Flagstaff
New York and her cement-cracked fingernails
Austin's legendarily stinky feet
bring me Billings, Montana (and the night Slayer played there)
bring me Texas's arterial language of freeways
bring me Maine's soft interest in its strangers
or just
bring me a Frontier Roll
& don't complain
if I sleep past eight o'clock.

On Wednesday I am leaving you
to crawl softly back along the tether
I found on my ankle a month ago.
If you love me, 'Burque,
you will kiss me once
like unexpected rain in the night
when I am not looking
or am already gone. ▪

Mikaela Renz

The Volunteers

Poet, mentor, teacher, and planner, Mikaela Renz was key in organizing the tremendous volunteer effort that made NPS 2005 possible. She continues to support the poetry community as a member of ABQ Slams and the International Poetry Institute, and by organizing events. Her passion for, and commitment to, poetry and Slam are invaluable to the community.

I was brought on in the homestretch of planning NPS to help organize volunteers. As Danny laid out the schedule of events for the four days, I wrote down how many volunteers we'd need—for sign in, for tickets, for setup, for breakdown—day events, eight venues a night, semifinals, finals, receptions, openings, readings—my spreadsheet grew and grew and grew, eventually requiring an eight-page printout that I updated daily and printed at the end of my duties for the night—somewhere between 2:00 and 4:00 a.m. during the event. Meanwhile the names of volunteers kept pouring in—by e-mail, by phone, through people telling the organizers they were ready to help. We knew that as soon as all the poets descended on Albuquerque, we'd have to plug them all into the volunteer holes.

Danny kept saying "bigger boat," but I didn't believe him until volunteer orientation the Sunday before the competition began. The room was packed to the gills with over one hundred folks. The poets were set to arrive the next day. While I'd planned to work my day job and join NPS at night, on day two I walked into my boss's office and said, "Things aren't going well. I can't be here. I've got to be there." From that moment, I dove in over my head.

On Wednesday, I got in a fight with one poet who wanted to volunteer at events that we already had filled up. "That's not fair," she cried. "What do you have left to volunteer for?" By the end of our negotiation, she was working enough to earn a much-coveted spot volunteering at the finals event.

Although it was overwhelming and exhilarating and ultimately exhausting, the buoyancy of excitement and palpable energy from poets and the community that poured out to fill the venues kept us all suspended without need of air. ■

Figure 14. Mikaela Renz and Eric Bodwell at NPS 2005. *Courtesy of David Huang*

Mikaela Renz
Holy Water

Science is beginning to confirm the power of the word. Mystics have known
for as long as man has been speaking that words have the power to literally
change the air we breathe, the water we drink, the experiences we can have.
Now, Masaru Emoto, a scientist in Japan, has shown that words—written
or spoken—shape water molecules. Words with good connotations create
symmetrical patterns; words like hate spawn asymmetry. This is only true of
unpolluted water.

I.
What cannot be purified
cannot be transformed:

what can be transformed
is pure;

thus is born a morality
of molecules,

holy water
of a weighted hand—

our words
at the center

or maybe the crystalline edge
of the great unknown,

where what we can control
and what we cannot fathom

dance together to the beat
of vibrating cosmic strings,

Moses parting the water
not with holy staff

but with a plea
(a command?).

Human voice
urging rearrangement:

water obeys
(responds?),

interprets the energy of his voice
into action,

miracle
made science,

law,
suggestion.

II.
One Jewish sect asserts the Torah itself is just the name of God—
one word that calls forth—embodies—inhabits creation.

Defaming that book
means calling forth darkness,

chaos,
nothingness,

known only to so-called
insurgents

who now sit praying
in American-run jails.

We torture flesh
and believe in freedom.

We protect our interests
without blaming our banks.

We speak in the dark,
create terror,

our words forming asymmetrical structures
in pools of pure blood.

What will transform this evil?
What purification is possible for twisting lies?

Most cleanliness
is removal of debris:

first
we jail the jailors,

sop up the blood,
tend to the wounds,

speak kindly to the hurt,
free the innocent,

burn the prison,
and pray

that our words will fall silent,
that our prayers for peace will rise,

part the waters,
connect what has been too-long divided,

let fall what may,
the heavy fruit of justice

hanging
in the tree of knowledge

we must all bite
and swallow. ▪

Jon Paszkiewicz

Making the Event Happen

Having skulked around the Slam scene prior to NPS, Jon decided to jump in headfirst as a volunteer, becoming so inspired that he started slamming with his own poetry, making it to the Albuquerque team finals in 2007 and receiving frequent invitations to perform at area schools.

Prior to the summer of 2005, I had never heard of or been to a Poetry Slam. I was writing some poetry but was spending most of my energy on essays and short stories, when someone heard a reading of some of my work and suggested that my style was suited for Slam. Nationals was about two weeks away, so I signed up as a volunteer. After the first day, I was driving a truck filled with folding chairs and volunteers, setting up doormen and security and working insane hours, just to get this thing off the ground. After hearing a lot of good work and seeing Team Albuquerque win, I went back to doing whatever it is that I do, not seeing Slam until flying out by myself on a whim to Austin for Nationals the following year. A month or so later I thought, "Maybe I should give this Slam thing a shot . . ." ▪

Jon Paszkiewicz
You Are the Snow

He is a pronoun
He is a pronoun and you are the snow
Not the snow that disappoints because it doesn't stick
And turns into dirty slush

You are the snow that will be a snowball
Or hold the shape of a footprint
Or anchor an icicle
But first
You have to paint the tops of the trees
Then the fence posts
Then the ground

And some of you will land in his mouth
Because he catches you with his tongue
Head held back
Nostrils to the sky
He catches you with his tongue because

He is a pronoun

And she is a pumpkin

He is a pronoun and she is a pumpkin
She grows in a field and you can paint her first
Because in her field there aren't any trees or fences or cars
Only her vine
It smells like pumpkin pie and pumpkin candles
And you paint her without footprints

He stands outside
Mouth agape
His parents were the Fourth of July and the Ocean
One of your flakes lands on his tongue
And it closes his mouth

And you keep snowing because
You're cancelling school and
You've got reasons that you haven't told them yet
But you're melting on his tongue

And she doesn't have trees in her field
But since no one can see her all of the time
All around her field, she grows pomegranates

She knows that they're sweet
She doesn't know how sweet
She's never eaten one because
She is a pumpkin

And she smells like November

You know that each one has a hundred seeds
Every one wrapped in her hopes for him

And

You paint them because
You are the snow
And you see her all the time
And you know

You sit on his tongue and he tastes
Tastes November
And pomegranate and smells pumpkin and starts walking
Past the cars
Beyond the fence posts
And through the trees because

He is a pronoun

. . . And he tastes her
You came to him and painted her on it
She is a pumpkin
And he is finding us to tell them
. . . You are holding his footprints and

Her vines touch his eyes

And

They both love Christmas.

Today,
There is no school because
You're painting him
Lying with November
She loves him and

They're both holding Christmas.

Chapter Five

NPS 2005 and the
ABQ Slam Team Champions' Story

After months of preparation, poets from seventy-five Slam teams from around the country began to descend on Albuquerque on Tuesday, August 9, 2005. Over the next four days, 20,000 people would attend at least one of the events, from day events at the National Hispanic Cultural Center, to semifinals on Friday night, to the final event on Saturday. The city was abuzz, and it was hard to go anywhere without hearing someone tell the story of this marvelous thing they went to last night called a Poetry Slam. For the poets, it was a nonstop reunion party punctuated by competition for points for poetry. What could be more fun? At the end, Team Albuquerque was declared National Team Champion, and Albuquerque proved itself as a city that comes out for poetry. ▮

Daniel S. Solis

Letter from the Chair of NPS 2005 (from the Event Program)

It was 1990, in Cambridge, Massachusetts. I walked into TT the Bear's Place and saw Patricia Smith performing her poetry. That night I didn't understand that my life had been changed forever. What I did know was that I was excited and intimidated and stunned by the small beautiful black woman with incredible poetry and gigantic stage presence. I knew I could never do what she did, but I hoped that I could, with enough hard work, find my own voice and do something similar—the same intensity with a different style. That night I began a journey that continues as you read this.

Then I learned about Poetry Slam, or to be more precise, I learned about the competitive side of Slam. I learned the rules and strategy and the history of Slam. I learned about memorization and discipline and mic technique. I learned about resonance, how to "capture a room" and how to "quiet a crowd" using nothing but the poem. But I had a long, long way to go before I really learned about the most important aspects of the Poetry Slam.

The most important things about Poetry Slam are things I am still learning, that Noah growled like a dinosaur while walking down the aisle as a ring bearer, that Mikaila likes dogs but thinks that cats are evil, that Corinna's passion for a certain tiny carnivorous dinosaur has cooled, that Wanda likes to sleep in the middle of the bed, that Sophia can stand on her own now.

It doesn't matter if you don't know what I'm talking about.

It only matters that you know this: the point is not the points, and sometimes the point isn't the poetry either.

Sometimes—all the time—the point is where the poetry comes from, from the lives that we slog or dance or just make it through somehow to get to each other and say, "Look! This, I lived this! I saw this! I dreamed this!" We spill forth onstage like flowers and whiskey and drums, lighting up the night for a moment with the gems we mined from the vast mountains of moments that brought us inexorably and finally here, here, together.

Poetry matters, Slam matters, but what matters more are the relationships we create and maintain. Poetry Slam brings us together, and sometimes we are gifted with friendships we wouldn't otherwise have known. Many of the friends I have made through the Poetry Slam are now more like family than friends. This second family makes my life richer and happier than I ever could have imagined; it is surely more than I deserve. And now, here we are, for these four days, at the largest National Poetry Slam in the history of the event. So poets, slammers, slam your asses off! Bring the most brilliant performance of your most inspired writing that the world has ever seen! Tear the proverbial "roof off the sucker!" Shine like white-hot miracles, like the brilliant fist of the sun.

But remember, the friends you make, the new family you are blessed with, the relationships you start now and cultivate over the years, these things will outlast anything you do onstage. This is your moment; this is your gift; this, my sisters and brothers, is the point. ■

Figure 15. Daniel S. Solis Hosting Indy Finals at NPS 2005. *Courtesy of David Huang*

ABQ Slams
NPS 2005 Schedule of Events

Time	Event	Location
Tuesday, August 9, 2005		
5:00–7:00 p.m.	Early Registration	National Hispanic Cultural Center (NHCC)
5:00–8:00 p.m.	Pre-NPS 2005 Welcome Party Hosted by *Albuquerque the Magazine*	NHCC Plaza Mayor
8:30–10:30 p.m.	Sneak Preview: *Hawaii Slam: Poetry in Paradise & Omaha's First*	NHCC Bank of America Theatre
Wednesday, August 10, 2005		
9:00–11:00 a.m.	Registration	Hotel Blue
Noon–2:00 p.m.	Opening Ceremonies	Robinson Park
2:00–3:30 p.m.	Pull the Next One Up (a.k.a. the Rookie Open Mic)	Robinson Park
7:00–11:00 p.m.	Bouts 1–16	See Tournament Bouts
11:00 p.m.–1:00 a.m.	Hip-Hop Headquarters	Disc-O
11:00 p.m.–1:00 a.m.	Erotic Poetry Reading	El Rey Theater
Thursday, August 11, 2005		
9:00 a.m.	Poetry of the Oppressed Workshop, Virginia Hampton	NHCC
10:30 a.m.	Preparing Poems for Performance Workshop, Paula Friedrich	NHCC
10:30 a.m.–Noon	Jewish Showcase	NHCC Wells Fargo Auditorium
10:30 a.m.–Noon	EC Challenge Survivor Slam	NHCC Under the Cottonwoods
Noon	48-Hour Open Mic Kickoff	Out ch'Yonda Performance Space
Noon–1:30 p.m.	The "Rainbow" Reading	NHCC Journal Theatre
12:30–2:30 p.m.	*Hawaii Slam: Poetry in Paradise & Omaha's First* Screenings	NHCC Bank of America Theatre
1:30–3:00 p.m.	African-American Showcase	NHCC Journal Theatre
3:00–4:30 p.m.	Asian-American Showcase	NHCC Bank of America Theatre
3:00–4:30 p.m.	Grief & Remembrance Reading	NHCC Wells Fargo Auditorium

3:00–4:30 p.m.	Nerd Slam	NHCC Under the Cottonwoods
7:00–11:00 p.m.	Bouts 16–32	See Tournament Bouts
11:00 p.m.–1:00 a.m.	Hip-Hop Headquarters	Disc-O
11:00 p.m.–1:00 a.m.	SlamMasters' Slam	El Rey Theater

Friday, August 12, 2005

9:00 a.m.	The Six Steps for Building Poetry, Laura E. J. Moran	NHCC
10:30 a.m.	The Feminine Voice in Political Poetry: How to Write a Political Poem Without Writing a Political Poem, Sarah McKinstry-Brown	NHCC
9:30–10:30 a.m.	Kids' Show	NHCC Under the Cottonwoods
10:00 a.m.–Noon	*Hawaii Slam: Poetry in Paradise & Omaha's First* Screenings	NHCC Bank of America Theatre
10:30 a.m.–Noon	World Peace Reading	NHCC Under the Cottonwoods
10:30 a.m.–1:00 p.m.	SlamMasters' Meeting	NHCC PNM Rehearsal Hall
Noon–1:30 p.m.	Women's Showcase	NHCC Journal Theatre
12:30–2:00 p.m.	Poetry Teaching Tips	NHCC Under the Cottonwoods
12:30–2:30 p.m.	*Word!* Screening	NHCC Bank of America Theatre
1:30–3:00 p.m.	Latino Showcase	NHCC Journal Theatre
3:00–4:30 p.m.	Indigenous Showcase	NHCC Bank of America Theatre
3:00–4:30 p.m.	Youth Slam	NHCC Wells Fargo Auditorium
3:00–4:30 p.m.	Group Piece Showcase	NHCC Under the Cottonwoods
7:00–11:00 p.m.	Semifinal Bouts	See Tournament Bouts
11:00 p.m.–1:00 a.m.	Indy Tournament	El Rey Theater

Saturday, August 13, 2005

10:30 a.m.–Noon	Slam Family Meeting	Hotel Blue Conference Room
11:00 a.m.–Noon	Open Mic Stage @ We Art the People Festival	Robinson Park
1:00–1:30 p.m.	Poet's Plaza Dedication	Harwood Art Center
1:30–3:00 p.m.	Head-to-Head Haiku	Harwood Art Center
3:00–5:30 p.m.	Slam Family Picnic	Tingley Field
8:00–11:30 p.m.	NPS 2005 Finals!	Kiva Auditorium

Shelle Luaces

The National Poetry Slam 2005 at the National Hispanic Cultural Center

Director of education, National Hispanic Cultural Center, Shelle Luaces was the winner of the 2007 Bravos Award for Arts Education.

For several days in August 2005, the theatres, patios, quiet corners, and pyramid-inspired stairs of the National Hispanic Cultural Center were filled with poets of all ages, writers from all cultural backgrounds, lovers of poetry and poet-lovers, and above all—words. Words in English, Spanish, and French were whispered, spoken, chanted, and sung. Words, rhythms, ideas, and voices moved off the pages of journals and chapbooks, filled the buildings, flowed onto the Plaza Mayor, and floated through the bosque and down the Rio Grande.

For the National Hispanic Cultural Center (NHCC), there was an obvious alignment between our mission and the work of the National Poetry Slam. We are committed to preserving, presenting, and promoting Latino arts and culture—and the poetry teams in New Mexico and across the country are filled with Latino voices. The NHCC opened its theatre doors to NPS 2005 because spoken word poetry is at its core about celebrating personal and cultural identity through the sharing of stories, thoughts, ideas, and passions. The National Poetry Slam 2005 connected poets to audiences, ideas to individuals, youth to community, and brought an incredible diversity of poets center stage at the National Hispanic Cultural Center. In the end, NPS 2005 was a living, unique, and dynamic manifestation of cultures—a perfect event for a cultural center.

The NHCC champions spoken word as an educational opportunity for youth because it is a powerful avenue for improving reading and writing skills and building confidence and presentation skills along with learning from and valuing diverse voices. NPS 2005 engaged youth in the community through workshops with local and visiting poets and many accessible (free and alcohol-free) poetry events. Spoken word poetry can simultaneously engage participants and presenters of all ages. Poetry slams encourage new artists and established artists to present side-by-side. Poetry slams are one of the rare cultural spaces where a teenager will share with, perform alongside, and listen to someone from the "over 35" category.

The NHCC supports spoken word poetry as a vital way to explore and share the human experience. It is immediate; it is personal. It is not media driven; instead it is driven by self-expression, individual creativity, and person-to-person communication. No large-screen plasma TV can replace the force of live performance. Increased broadband access will never surpass the power of words and voice passionately choreographed.

As the director of education at the National Hispanic Cultural Center, it was a pleasure and an honor to support the National Poetry Slam 2005 in Albuquerque. I cherish poetry on and off the page and believe in supporting the voice of poets—knowing their poems promote, preserve, and present culture outside the walls of any cultural center and beyond the start and end of a poetry event. Spoken word poetry and the National Poetry Slam were definitely at home on the stages at the NHCC—but, spoken word poetry can be at home in a small courtyard, in the corner of a coffee shop, or wherever a poet's words and metaphors can roll, swirl, and beat their way into the ears and thoughts of an audience. ■

"*The National Poetry Slam 2005 was one of the highlights of NHCC's programming to date. NPS 2005 filled our theatres with a large, enthusiastic, and diverse audience. For many it was their first visit but* not *their last!*"

—Joseph Anthony Wasson Jr.,
NHCC Theatre Programmer/Production Manager

Figure 16. Poets Swarming the National Hispanic Cultural Center at NPS 2005. *Courtesy of David Huang*

Shappy

Nerd Slam under the Cottonwoods

Hello. My name is Shappy. I'm a nerd, and I'm pretty proud of that!

I've been doing the Nerd Slam since 2002. I had realized that the National Poetry Slam is not that different than a Star Trek convention, only instead of Borgs and Klingons fighting over trading cards, you get poets fighting over score creep and time penalties. So, why not seal the deal and see if the nerds of spoken word could step up and show off their geek knowledge?

The Nerd Slam isn't a "traditional" slam. There are no scores, no time penalties, and props are definitely allowed (especially lightsabers!). It's evolved into more of a poetic trivia-off. While group pieces and girls get a free pass, all other nerd poets go head to head in a trivia Thunderdome to

Figure 17. Nerd Slam under the Cottonwoods at NPS 2005. *Courtesy of David Huang*

see which nerd gets to perform their "Ode to Boba Fett"! Two poets enter; one poet leaves!

At the 2005 Albuquerque National Poetry Slam, my cohost Robbie Q. Tefler and I had a blast hosting under the cottonwoods (or as I called it "The Shire") and thankfully no nerds suffered sunburn or heat exhaustion! Quite a feat, considering over two hundred nerds, geeks, and dweebs showed up to perform, support, or heckle their sci-fi and comic book–loving brethen!

The following poem is what I used to win the 2005 Albuquerque National Poetry Slam SlamMasters' Slam! A victory for all nerdy slammers! I now share that title with my girlfriend Cristin O'Keefe Aptowicz who founded the NYC-Urbana Poetry Slam that I now run.

May the force be with you! ■

Shappy

George Bush,
Please stop the war,
Because I hate it.
I hate the war.
I hate all wars
Except for *Star Wars*,
Which totally RULES!
Like a dictator rules,
Which is what you are, George,
A dick-tater.
You are evil, like Darth Vader
But you don't look as cool as Darth Vader.
He wore a black masklike death,
Which is what you are, George,
Death.
You wear a mask to hide your evil,
Only it is not as cool and shiny as Darth Vader's.
It is chipped and dented
Like the Millenium Falcon.
Han Solo used to drive the Millenium Falcon
Until Boba Fett turned him in to Jabba the Hutt
for a bounty.
Jabba the Hutt is a fat, slimy businessman who lives
in a cave
Like Dick Cheney.
Jabba the Hutt surrounded himself with bounty hunters
and evil robots and naked alien chicks
Just like you and Dick Cheney.
George Bush doesn't care about sand people!
And I hate to ruin the whole *Star Wars* Trilogy for you,
George, but in the end—the evil empire is toppled!
And although I bet you are thinking I am talking about
Iraq, I'm actually talking about YOU and your

administration, George!

The rebels win, George!

Those stupid peace-loving rebels WIN!

And you can appoint as many Jar Jar Binks as you want in the

Senate, but it's not gonna stop the rebels from

WINNING!

We got Yoda on our side, bitch!

All you got is some smelly old man in a robe who kills

people—like your dad!

Which is why I love *Star Wars*

But not wars in general.

So please—stop the war. ■

Paula Friedrich

Albuquerque Nationals

Poet Paula Friedrich knows the pain and glory of organizing a National Poetry Slam from Nationals in Seattle in 2001. She held a daytime workshop at the NHCC during Nationals 2005 sponsored by A Room of Her Own Foundation.

I didn't come to Albuquerque as much as Albuquerque came to me—like a hot, dry powder with the distinct tones of gasoline, minerals, and *queso*, but otherwise defying description. My mother moved us to the city after our family had lived in North Carolina for nearly a decade: going from abundant forest to stark expanse and highways was quite an initial shock. But the landscape gradually reached into me like a divine hand, showing me the beauty of singular objects and creatures—layered rocks, turtles, owls, gnarly sticks—against the vast backdrop of sand and sky in ways that I had never perceived before.

While writer's block comes and goes like a stubborn whale diving deep into the unknown for years before resurfacing, dry spells of the creative kind were never a problem for me in Albuquerque. From first arriving there in 1989 to teaching workshops at the National Poetry Slam there in 2005, Albuquerque is the place I return to for lyrical water. I can't say why, unless it's the fact that it's the only place I can have a cup of coffee with every star in the universe, inhale enough green chile to heal the soul, and have a decent conversation with light, clouds, and earth. ■

Paula Friedrich
Panning for Teeth

Against the Rio Grande, my feet are ice blocks
under the boulder weight of a box screen.

To find bones other than ancient horse teeth
would offer someone their shot at fame:

The task ignores a mineral bosque dawn
where the white owl we startled has escaped. ▪

Matthew John Conley

Head-to-Head Haiku

I had wanted the Head-to-Head Haiku Championship for years. My Slam friends & I had long vied with haiku—nasty & irreverent & yet somehow beautiful & beholden to the art of poetry war. Bragging rights & a quiet fortitude in five-seven-five madness were the only trophies, yet our hunger for the National Championship knew no bounds. Onstage in the basement of the Harwood Art Center, amidst the mountain air ghosts & memories I had walked so many moons amongst, I looked out into the familiar faces of friends & family in my old hometown & offered my own three lines to Honor the House & raise the roof laughter like a stained-glass castle. It felt oh-so-good to accomplish my dream in Albuquerque, mother of my mouth, the place I first opened my own & spoke seventeen syllables of sagebrush. Outside afterward, former champion Ed Mabry said to me, "Welcome to the club." I told him, "You don't want me in this club!" We both smiled & slapped hands & nodded our heads heavenward. ▪

Matthew John Conley
Haiku

Some poets write good
poetry, but all poets
write bad poetry. ▪

Virginia Hampton

Forty-Eight-Hour Poetry Jook Joint . . . Out ch'Yonda

Albuquerque transplant from the Southeast, cofounder of Out ch'Yonda, a performance space on Fourth Street in Albuquerque's historic Barelas neighborhood, and cohost of both the Poetry of the Oppressed Workshop and the Kids' Show at the National Hispanic Cultural Center during NPS 2005.

When my partner, Stef, and I found out the National Poetry Slam was coming to Albuquerque, and that it would be taking place mostly between the KiMo and other venues downtown and the National Hispanic Cultural Center, we realized that we would be strategically situated right in the middle of these two areas—the perfect spot for some poetry lunacy. We asked Danny Solis how we could participate in the Slam of 2005, and he said he'd get back to us. A few days later, Danny asked if we wanted to do a forty-eight-hour poetry event. We said, "Sure." Danny looked at us again with a furrowed brow and asked, "Are you sure you understand what we mean?" Clearly, we did not. Forty-eight hours meant a nonstop poetry open mic at Out ch'Yonda. It meant that we would not be sleeping much for about two days.

As someone who is not unfamiliar with both psychedelics and college finals, for me being awake for two days wasn't such a hard thing to imagine. But to keep our art space open for that long took planning, coffee, patience, coffee, and a lot of poets to host, and coffee. The poets, two per shift, took on the sixteen three-hour spots and kept poetry going from the beginning 'til the wee hours. Highlights included Sina Soul and To, a French Beat Box poet and the winner of the French Slam in 2004. His prize was a plane ticket to the next slam, which just happened to be in Albuquerque. He came early in the event and kept returning throughout. At one hazy point in the a.m., I remember him, Sina (who speaks like five languages and sings like a freight train), Muni (an amazingly skinny violinist), and a few other people drumming, reciting poetry in at least three languages, and jamming for nearly the whole three-hour session.

We beckoned to the poets who passed by every hour or so en route from downtown to the NHCC and invited them in to participate in the moment at hand. Poets came by for some inspiration before going to work, and at the end we took a nap, got up again, and feasted on waffles on Sunday afternoon. It was beautiful. And the fact that the black population of Albuquerque doubled that weekend was something to write home to my mother about, let me tell ya! We also conducted a poetry performance workshop, and I performed at a youth treatment center. The only thing we didn't get to do was actually attend any of the National Slam!

On the regular, Out ch'Yonda Live ArtZ Space usually is home to a multiethnic experimental theatre company called OmniRootZ, a gallery, a radical bookstore, La Semilla, KoolKatz Children's Ensemble, Aparna's Yoga classes, and on the weekends we distribute food to friends, neighbors, and anyone else who walks by or needs a fresh bell pepper or a sandwich. We are grassroots, neither a nonprofit nor a for-profit, and we do art "by any means necessary." This poetry event seemed just like our cup of coffee. It was an honor to have participated in what may be Albuquerque's most shining moment in the art world. We were so inspired that we continue the tradition every April for National Poetry Month.

Many thanks to all who made this madness possible. Keep it coming! ▪

Gene Grant

Albuquerque Slam

No way. No way, no how did this kid, a long way under six feet with a swagger out of proportion to his stature, just step inside the circle. I think I made a noise when it happened, a combination of a low groan and anxiety.

The circle was on the corner of Central and Fifth, not two blocks from the El Rey, where two nights later during the semifinals the Albuquerque team put everyone on notice that maybe, just maybe, our team was headed for something special.

It was a cipher, a beautifully impromptu moment when poets, rappers, and other craftsmen and women of the spoken word have at it, slamming rhymes, lyrics, and anything else at each other for the surrounding crowd's approval. Winners are "chosen" almost purely on how effectively opponents are buried under the beauty of their words, style, and confidence. You stay as long as you keep winning, according to the crowd, and along the way, the dramatic stakes skyrocket. How long they last depends on how much creative stamina, bravado, and the opponent's breaking point lasts.

A poet from Philadelphia had been summarily dismissing any and all challengers for a solid thirty minutes, and challengers were becoming hard to find. This guy was a beast—young, gifted, and black. And swinging it. He was enjoying himself.

This was going to be ugly.

It was Wednesday night of the 2005 National Poetry Slam in Albuquerque, New Mexico, a city, to the laymen, that had no business hosting an event with seventy-five other Slam poet teams from around the country. And a few from other countries to boot.

On that corner, at that moment—about two in the morning—the very idea of winning the event was very far past a long shot. And this Hispanic kid was about to prove it.

And so, here we were. My friend Darryl and I, in the circle, about to watch this Albuquerque kid take on Goliath. But a funny thing happened on that sidewalk. That fear of an Albuquerque Embarrassment in the face of a big-city interloper who must, *must*, be better, only because he was from somewhere else, soon turned into a wild cacophony of cheering as it became more and more clear he had game. Serious game.

That kid, whoever shorty was, trounced him. Convincingly.

It's with no small amount of guilt I speak of the moment. I've reflected on it a ton over time, trying, trying to get a handle on just why I caved so quickly. I've also discussed it with a few trusted friends, and the conclusion is actually rather simple.

It's about self-image. Not mine, but Albuquerque's. It's about living in a city well described by author V. B. Price as "a city at the end of the world." Things happen out on the edge. Sometimes glorious but unseen, other times you're damned glad no one was here to witness it.

It's Albuquerque's dilemma or opportunity, depending on your point of view. Let me put it this way; after almost twenty years here and sucked in by any number of "next big things" for Albuquerque that amounted to *bubkes*, you start to lose faith. The internal voices of doubt can go from a nagging whisper to incredibly loud. The clues to greatness are all around, but why have we never been "seen"? Maybe we're not as creative as we hold ourselves. That can't be right, can it? Maybe we're all so emotionally exhausted from propping up icons from generations ago, we're hopelessly lost in the forest of *curanderas*, watercolors of Abiquiu landscapes, and pottery for the postmodern trees.

Dilemma or opportunity? When you toil in obscurity, you can never be sure where you stand.

So maybe, just maybe, what four young men and one even younger woman from this city did in one fell swoop was grab this city by the shirt and drag it kicking and screaming across the national threshold into our first Postmodern Moment.

And it only took four days, at least in real time. In reality, what becomes apparent when you root around poetry circles is that victory was a culmination of faiths—some large, some barely there, but faith nonetheless.

These kids are lucky. They have not watched this city flail away at perception windmills for twenty years. They could care less. They're poets. They just do. And they have been doing, with leadership, fearlessness, and yes, faith, as their guide.

Albuquerque winning the 2005 National Poetry Slam, on the other hand, proved convincingly that there was more walk to the talk, as inspiring as it's been in coffee shops, church basements, and bars.

What was happening in those Albuquerque nooks, unseen to most, was profound. These kids were designing their own rules of engagement with the world around them without permission or approval from an older generation afraid of its own creative shadow and paralyzed by disappointment.

Legacies are a tough consideration. It takes time, sometimes a very long time to assess what

Figure 18. Sold-Out Box Office for Finals Night NPS 2005. *Courtesy of David Huang*

the long-term impacts are on a culture. These things can be fleeting, and at the end of the day, a confection, like your home city sports team winning a championship. After the parades, rings, and T-shirts are sold, what?

For me the 2005 National Poetry Slam win was and will be a seminal moment in the city's arc—a glorious and long-lasting flare launched over the consciousness of a city that said "we're OK," and took a full-on black/brown youth-centered hit.

The poetry community here has literally lifted two segments of society—people of color and a younger generation—to another level single-handedly. Flip it to (Slam) poetry to take two segments of the city culture to the top tier in a city-to-city nationwide competition. This is no small accomplishment. It happened organically, in its own pace and scale and purely through art, not a goal of making a magazine list of some sort.

That it came from five kids, not a one over thirty-five years old, and kicked off for me by one brave soul on a street corner, made it all the sweeter. ▪

Barbara Grothus

A Poetic Audience Perspective

It was an accident. I saw
my neighbor. He mentioned
the crowd. I snapped.

Ran over without a penny, even
For a cuppa. How could I not?
I was Right There.

I met parents. Here
from Hawaii, just off
the plane. Their son, his team.

The kids were Hot, on
Fire. Their words
like sparks
Flying. But very precise.

My first time, I won!
A pass on KUNM.
I went slamming.
Every night.

Raw, cutting, biting, tragic. Clear.
And Funny.

Whole Array, slam bingo
Not unlike rain, train, pain, momma,
And jail.

But better. All week.

Lucky me. I remember.

ABQ Slams
Tournament Bouts

Wednesday, August 10, 2005				
VENUES	**7:00 p.m.**		**9:00 p.m.**	
	TEAMS	STORM	TEAMS	STORM
LAUNCHPAD	Noraz Miami Corpus Christi St. Louis Central NJ	Karrie Waarala	Worcester Denver Hollywood Columbus Austin	Panika Dillon
GOLDEN WEST	NYC Louder Arts Albuquerque Oneonta France Milwaukee	Buddy Wakefield	Pittsburgh Madison Atlanta Farmington Baton Rouge	Teresa Driver
FLYING STAR	LA Green Winter Park Palatine Durham Montevallo	Darrell Payne	Brooklyn Hawaii Mesa Newark, NJ Providence	Miller George
Nat'l Inst. Flamenco	Bowling Green Oklahoma City Delray Beach Sacramento Eugene	Anis Mojgani	Seattle Dallas Rockford Ft. Worth Winston-Salem	Elizabeth Thomas
GORILLA TANGO (Main)	San Antonio Berkeley Detroit New Orleans Orlando	Joshua Fleming	Omaha Oakland Santa Fe Vancouver Boston Cantab	David Schein
GORILLA TANGO (Loft)	Newark, DE San Jose Minneapolis DC/Baltimore Houston	Ragan Fox	Boston Lizard Lounge Salt Lake City Kalamazoo Ann Arbor Ithaca	Jus Caus
OPM	Las Vegas Chicago MG NYC-Urbana Taos Charlotte	The Mo-Man	South Florida Modesto Chicago G Mill San Francisco Palo Alto	Aaron Trumm
EL REY			Colorado Springs NYC Nuyorican Columbia, SC Flint Normal	Zork

Thursday, August 11, 2005				
VENUES	**7:00 p.m.**		**9:00 p.m.**	
	TEAMS	**STORM**	**TEAMS**	**STORM**
LAUNCHPAD	Colorado Springs Vancouver, Canada Dallas Baton Rouge Kalamazoo	Jus Caus	San Antonio Oneonta Charlotte Winter Park Sacramento	Karrie Waarala
GOLDEN WEST	NYC Nuyorican Boston Cantab Rockford Brooklyn Ann Arbor	Aaron Trumm	New Orleans Las Vegas Corpus Christi Montevallo San Jose	Anis Mojgani
FLYING STAR	Santa Fe Seattle Farmington Salt Lake City Austin	Zork	Orlando Chicago MG St. Louis Bowling Green Minneapolis	Buddy Wakefield
Nat'l Inst. Flamenco	Normal Chicago G Mill Pittsburgh Newark, NJ Denver	David Schein	Detroit Milwaukee Miami Durham Newark, DE	The Mo-Man
GORILLA TANGO (Main)	Omaha San Francisco Madison Providence Hollywood	Elizabeth Thomas	NYC Louder Arts NYC-Urbana Central NJ Oklahoma City DC/Baltimore	Darrell Payne
GORILLA TANGO (Loft)	Flint Modesto Winston-Salem Mesa Worcester	Teresa Driver	Berkeley France Noraz Palatine Eugene	Ragan Fox
OPM	Oakland Palo Alto Atlanta Boston Lizard Lounge Columbus	Miller George		
EL REY	Columbia, SC South Florida Ft. Worth Hawaii Ithaca	Panika Dillon	Albuquerque Taos LA Green Delray Beach Houston	Joshua Fleming

VENUE	LAUNCHPAD	GOLDEN WEST	FLYING STAR	NHCC
Friday, August 12, 2005				
8:00 p.m. Showcases				
SHOWCASES	HEAD 2 HEAD HAIKU	GROUP PIECE	GROUP PIECE	NONE
9:00 p.m. Team Semis				
TEAMS	Ft. Worth	San Francisco	Boston Lizard Lounge	NYC Louder Arts
	Palo Alto	Charlotte	Seattle	Hawaii
	Berkeley	Detroit	Baton Rouge	Albuquerque
	Mesa	DC/Baltimore	Hollywood	Oakland
	NYC-Urbana	Minneapolis	LA Green	Delray Beach

Friday, August 12, 2005		
VENUES	8:00 p.m. Showcases	9:00 p.m. Team Semis
LAUNCHPAD	HEAD 2 HEAD HAIKU	Ft. Worth
		Palo Alto
		Berkeley
		Mesa
		NYC-Urbana
GOLDEN WEST	GROUP PIECE	San Francisco
		Charlotte
		Detroit
		DC/Baltimore
		Minneapolis
FLYING STAR	GROUP PIECE	Boston Lizard Lounge
		Seattle
		Baton Rouge
		Hollywood
		LA Green
NHCC	NONE	NYC Louder Arts
		Hawaii
		Albuquerque
		Oakland
		Delray Beach

Saturday, August 13, 2005			
	VENUE: KIVA AUDITORIUM		
	CHAMPIONSHIP COMPETITION		FEATURES
	TEAMS	POETS	
INDIVIDUALS CHAMPIONSHIP	Storm Seattle Boston Cantab San Francisco Ft. Worth Storm Baton Rouge	Anis Mojgani Christa Bell Eric Darby Jaime Kennedy Janean Livingston Ragan Fox Xero Skidmore	Buddy Wakefield (Storm) Sonya Renee (DC/Baltimore)
TEAM CHAMPIONSHIP	Albuquerque	Aaron Cuffee Carlos Contreras Hakim Bellamy Kenn Rodriguez	Team Hawaii Team France
	Charlotte	Bluz Maze Forever Mekkah Q Queen Sheba	
	Ft. Worth	Chuck Jackson Janean Livingston K.A. Williams Michael Guinn Stephen Sargent	
	Hollywood	Crystal Irby Javon Johnson Ratpack Slim Rives Simply Cat	

Pilote le Hot
Soweto-Aubervilliers
Member of the French Federation of Slam Poetry from Paris, Pilote le Hot
was on one of two international teams at NPS 2005.

Les mômes du Mozambique et ceux du Zimbabwe
Kids in Mozambique and Zimbabwe

Veulent les mêmes choses que ceux d'Aubervilliers
Want the same thing as those in my neighborhood

Les girafes d'leurs grands pères crocodiles et éléphants
The giraffes of their ancestors the crocodiles the elephants

S'trimballent dans des réserves pour touristes maintenant
Are confined to tourist reservations

Les lascars d'mon quartier se tapent d'la tour eiffel
Guys in my neighborhood don't care about the Eiffel Tower

Comme ceux des township s'foutent des troupeaux de gazelles
Just as those in townships don't give a damn about antelopes

Fument des cigarettes blondes boivent du coca cola
It's smokes and cokes

D' Joburg à Harare d' Lusaka à Tana
From Joburg to Harare, from Lusaka to Antananarivo

Leur café est trop clair mais dès l'début du jour
Their coffee's weak but when the sun comes up

C'est les mêmes débris d'verre que ceux d'en bas d'ma tour
It's the same broken bottles as in my project

Un disque de 50 Cents copié sur un ordi
A fifty-cent record burned on a PC

Passe de main en main autour d'un bout d'teushi
Passes from hand to hand along with a joint

A six heures du matin l'soleil d'la vie en rose
At 6 a.m. the sun goes up on the easy life

Donne à chacun son ombre et propose la même chose
Giving everyone a shadow and the same old routine

Les mômes du Zimbabwe savent que l' tango est mort
Kids in Zimbabwe know that the tango's dead

Qu' c' est l' argent qui décide du nom d' l' aéroport
That the airport is named after money instead

Z' en ont marre de marchander ou alors pour gagner
They're tired of haggling to make a buck

Comme ceux d' Aubervilliers les mômes du Zimbabwe
The kids in my 'hood and those of Zimbabwe

Tous les jours l' prince charmant pour les filles de là bas
Play prince charming for the local girls

A défaut d' cheval blanc porte les dernières Puma
Not on a white horse but in brand-new Nikes

Les chutes de Victoria ou Les volcans d'Auvergne
Victoria Falls or the Cote d'Azur

L' jour où on s' marriera on ira une semaine
We'll go there on our honeymoon for sure

Y veulent devenir des stars connaître la gloire et vite
They wanna be stars, attain quick fame

Des awards des cesars surfer dans l' vent d' la street
Win championships and Oscars, hang out on the avenue

Les mères célibataires les enfants d' divorcés
Single mothers with divorced parents

Les mêmes sœurs les mêmes frères jusqu'à Aubervilliers
The same sisters and brothers as we've got here

Quand le taux d' change varie la roue tourne un petit peu
The wheel turns slightly with the exchange rate

D' Soweto à Paros les mêmes règles du jeu
From Soweto to Paris the same rules apply

C' est le même message dans les mêmes écouteurs
It's the same message through the same earphones

Sur le même échiquier y jouent les mêmes couleurs
On the same chessboard, with the same pieces

Maman quand j' serai grand je veux devenir vivant
When I grow up Mama I wanna be alive

Plus m' ennuyer tout l' temps je n' ai pas d' autres plans
And not bored all the time I have no other plans

Les mômes du Zimbabwe comme ceux d' Aubervilliers
The kids in Zimbabwe and those in my neighborhood

Sont pas là pour payer l' loyer du monde entier
Pay rent for the entire world

Z' ont connu l' rockn'roll et la fée électrique
They know rock music and the electric fairy

D' Harare à Lagos d' Calvi à Rekjavik
From Harare to Lagos, from Rome to Helsinki

L' exeption culturelle elle espas politique
Protecting culture has nothing to do with politics

Mais à coté d' l' ombrelle un peu eurocentrique
So that next to the concerns of Eurocentrics

Les mômes du Zimbabwe comme ceux d' Aubervilliers
Kids in Zimbabwe and in my neighborhood

Parlent la même langue ont des airs coutumiers
Speak the same language and wear the same clothes

Sur tout l' globe un seul slang pour tout équilibrer
The slang's the same throughout the globe

Y z' ont les mêmes codes presque la même monnaie
They've got the same PIN codes, almost the same money

J' veux pas qu' ces mots deviennent un autre carnet d voyage
I don't want my words to be just a travelog

J' laisse la valse à Vienne l' moulin rouge à Paname
Vienna can have its waltzes and Paris its Pigalle

En shona en swaïli en verlan bienvenue
Welcome in Shona in Swahili and in our own slang

Maintenant que tout a un prix j' suis fier d' être de la rue
Now that money talks I'm proud to come from the 'hood

Maintenant que tout a un prix j' suis fier d' être de la rue
Now that money talks I'm proud to come from the 'hood

Rachel McKibbens
Your Best Behavior
SlamMaster from New York, Rachel McKibbens is a member of the
PSi Executive Council and was a member of the New York City Louder
Arts team at NPS 2005.

For the first time in twenty-two years, you recognize
your brother as a man. Boom. There he is:
standing in a puddle of blood in the kitchen.
His voice becomes a buzzard flying
circles above your neck. He has the lips
of an astronaut. The shoulders
you once sat upon now reveal a secret,

confessing their obscene beauty to you
in the hallway. There is no longer a sweetness
in praising the enormity of his hands.
You're not sure how much more of him you can take.

Every glance across the dinner table, each
accidental brush of his leg against yours
drags you further from the young catastrophes
you once were; the shared bed in winters,
the magnified deaths of burning ants, the belt buckle
that kissed your backs, Easter morning
in the basement with a stolen bottle of gin.

It is the last night you ever spend in that house.
For the next eight years, its only signs of you
are birthday cards on the mantel and a wreath
of pinecones made in Sunday school.
When your mother dies of a terrible disease,
you send a modest arrangement of snapdragons
and baby's breath.

All the men you sleep with become a quiet revenge
against the beautiful man you've been married to
since you were five. It is a polished infidelity,
an almost odorless betrayal.

That same year, you cut off your hair and quit your job.
Lose your apartment. Get addicted to coke.
Everything you need to live a soft, invisible life.
On your thirty-first birthday, you leave your car
on the side of the road and run into the empty dark.

Eventually, you find an ordinary town to die in.
Marry the first man who hits you. Buy a dog
that shits on the carpet. Give birth
to four ungrateful boys.

When you finally die, it is the best day of your life.
The doctor makes the announcement and leaves
the room. You are lying in bed, surrounded
by your sons and their agreeable wives.

It is very charming, they think, how your grandchild,
a stringy little girl with messy hair,
lays her head upon your chest,
listening for a heart
that has not been home in years. ■

Christa Bell

For Bashir

Christa Bell was a member of the Seattle team at NPS 2005.

I.

I've been
Waiting to hold yr feet in my lap
Since I saw them
& to kiss the tear tattooed on
yr face
to pull yr fingers over my
heart/just to see what they'd do &
watch you with all the eyes I can
gather
I want to get close enough to taste
How the water you would share
Holds my tongue until
If anybody asks me/where I'm going
I can say
With her

II.

The smell of me on vibrating plastic/chasing
Yr tongue through lavender dreamscapes
Confuses to   silence
Familiar fantasy of
Rough hands/torn panties/ gagged
Mouth/burning flesh

Your mouth floats just above mine and all you do
Is breathe   out
Raining wet/I   breathe back &
This is how we enter each other   quiet
As meditation
Urgent/as lovers

Equal as comrades
Sanctified
& free
no
pornography bred gorilladick/slamming in & out
of faceless pink cunt
just two thirsty women
drinking each other's breath
I press my hips harder into the
Buzzzzzzzzzing
Pieces of me rise up to meet you
This moon that is my heart breaks
Open/begins to weep
& I come
sucking my own fingers
stroking
the thought of you

III. (and yet)
Something about you is a closed door
And a little girl crying for her mommy
My
Hand between my legs can't silence this reality & it feels almost obscene to have you
& her in the same room
Together
Are we a   tragic/retelling of the color purple set in this millennium where
Shattered mothers replace/pa and Mr. _____

If so/I guess that makes you Nettie/ who escapes over oceans & into strange
Languages
Inside yr own head

Bringing an imposed gospel that you really can't believe into
Foreign lands
& i
I am Celie/excavating her own scriptures deep in the temple of her being

& this separation
this great chasm between us
will it be filled with years of questions & unanswered letters?
Silent disappearings & conversations with a god who you say
Keeps calling you home?

I have secrets & kisses I've been holding all my life for you

Come on & meet me in the field of lavender poppies
When
You're no longer inclined to smoke them

I'll be there waiting
In this lifetime or the next
Waiting
For you
To get it together
Girl
Just
Get it
Together ■

Editors

Individual Championship—2005

The majority of poets who compete in the indy competition come from receiving high scores for individual poems they perform as part of the team competition. That's right, not only are the teams' scores meticulously recorded and calculated bout by bout, the scores received by each individual poet are also tallied.

NPS 2005 was the last tournament that PSi allowed individual poets to enter. PSi called these lone wolves "Storm" poets to honor the late Pat Storm, a member of the Asheville NPS Championship team from 1995. These poets were woven into early bouts, and the high-scorers made it to indy semifinals on Friday night against individual poets from competing teams. PSi has now moved this entire indy championship to its own event, Individual World Poetry Slam (IWPS), which typically takes place in February.

In Albuquerque, fifteen Storm poets competed for the indy championship, including three who made it to the finals stage—Ragan Fox, Buddy Wakefield, and Anis Mojgani. Indy poets from the team competition included Eric Darby from Boston Cantab, Jamie Kennedy from San Francisco, Christa Bell from Seattle, Xero Skidmore from Baton Rouge, and Janean Livingston of Ft. Worth. For the final, Anis Mojgani went three tie-breaker rounds with Janean Livingston before they agreed to share the title. ■

Ragan Fox

Visiting and Competing in NPS 2005

Storm poet who competed for the Individual Championship at NPS 2005, Ragan Fox currently lives in Long Beach, California.

I have performed poetry in Albuquerque on two occasions, namely a regional competition called the Southwest Shootout and the 2005 National Poetry Slam. In both encounters, I felt as if a magical hand lifted me from the restricting and mechanical confines of a poetry cabaret to an arena in which audience members appeared to be genuinely invested in creativity as a mode of social activism. Directly after performing, poets and audience members native to Albuquerque engaged me in meaningful conversations about the themes present in my work, including gay rights, hate crime legislation, protesting the war in Iraq, and suburban malaise. Performance poetry should incite conversations about complex social phenomena. Albuquerque poets and audience members exemplify this obligation, a commitment that I believe is central to the aesthetic contract between performers and audience members. ■

Figure 19. Ragan Fox Competing for Indy Finals at NPS 2005. *Courtesy of David Huang*

Ragan Fox
Headstone

Fucking him was like *Waiting for Godot*;
he never came and I was happy when it ended.
I may be gay, **Jay**, but I don't play lay games with men who send out an
"ooh-baby, baby, what can *you* do for *me*?" vibe;
frankly, **Frank**, I would rather be bored and single than paired and annoyed.
I don't give a flying fuck if it doesn't "feel the same" with it on, **Jon**;
Jim's jimmy best be wrapped lest he inspire me to
cut it off
at the sac.

This message of appropriate massage is dedicated to all the Jays, Franks, Jims, Jons,
        Jerrys,
Steves, Sams, and Sylvesters who screw their souls into their own coffins.
Two decades of AIDS education goes swirling down a vacuous drain in the Bates motel
        because a condom clasps **Dick's** dick,
wraps itself like a straight jack-et around his shaft as he expects me to back-it up.
My brother-lover, apathy and AIDS are two words that don't belong in the same
        sentence.

I punctuate this moment in history
because we have been duped by dopes into believing three-letter words are less powerful
        than four;
HIV-fuck me,
we have forgotten that there's a quilt large enough to swallow cities,
gobble up yellow brick roads, trick us into warmth, steal the water from Dorothy
        before she throws it on the Wicked Witch of West Hollywood,
but rainbows bend, my friend;
we pop our eyes into compliance and a reliance on drugs to bury in our head the
        number of men and women dead,
as we lay in our bed,
send lusty looks,
and pretend we're livin' in 1970s disco Technicolor San Francisco.
But, boy, save your stupid bet;
I don't gamble with uncertain sex—

I will not forget or let any lover convince me that he's a wizard instead of a man
    behind a curtain.
In 2003, I, after a decade of not testing anything but the limits of my own sanity,
learned that I was HIV—
only a single day after finding out that a man I love and adore will live his life branded
by the gay scarlet "A";
I've tried to believe in justice,
but the world started lookin' a lot less blue that day,
lost its hue and beauty.
HIV and me will never be fair pairs or a couplet at the end of a Swan Song gone wrong.

I have spent days running trembling fingertips over lymph nodes praying that they
    don't turn into Braille;
hell, for ten years I confused my skinny frame for pulling the card of death from the tarot,
Pharaohs singing soothsaying whispers to me as I fuck one last time without caring
    about the risks;

those days are gone Jon, Jay, Frank, Jim, Jerry, Steve, Sam, and Sylvester;
I will wrap myself in the quilt, respect the living and remember the dead—
because (no) head (is worth its weight in) stone. ■

Anis Mojgani

Being the National Poetry Individual Champion

Co-winner of the Individual Championship at NPS 2005 from Portland, Oregon.

The morning after the 2005 National Poetry Slam, I rode to Texas, watching out the window the flat earth turn dark, beside me a trophy for being the number one Slam poet in the country. Sheesh.

Ten years before, I sat in the sun of my bedroom reading an article about Poetry Slam. I read a poem that describes the wind being like mustangs. It breathes. More than I knew poetry could. I breathe with it, and the breaths begin to shape me.

Marc Smith's "For the Little Guy." "The Invisible Man." Lisa Buscani's "A Prayer." I am smitten. Listening on repeat to Patricia Smith's "Undertaker." Jeffrey McDaniel perched onstage like a badger. Inspired to read poems out loud to no one but the bathroom walls because it is the only audience there. For no reason other then my gut tells me to.

Ten years later, I wake in Albuquerque with no voice, preparing to be part of this thing I have been shaped by. Preparing to find the hopes I have spent years inside of, being drawn for me by the eyes of 2,300 people.

Two days after finals, I get up at 3:30 p.m. While walking to KFC, I write a poem about the bones of angels. I smile. I won. I am no one. I am king of the world, and nobody knows my face. I am as special as you are. Go us. The tops of hotels have snowflakes sleeping on them, and the mountains of New Mexico are beautiful.

Anis Mojgani
for those who can still ride an airplane for the first time

I'm twenty-nine years old and am trying to figure out most days what being a man
    means
I don't drink fight or fuck
but these days I find myself wanting to do all three
and I don't really have a favorite color anymore
but I did when I was a kid and back then that color was blue
and back then
I wanted to be an architect an artist an astronaut a secret agent
a ranger for the world wildlife fund
and a hobo
when I was six years old or so I used to always throw my clothes
into my blue and yellow
plastic vinyl
Hot Wheels
car carrying suitcase
and run away
to beneath the dining room table

I've made out with more girls than I wish I've had
and not nearly as many as I'd like to
I've been in love four or five times
so I doubt I'm gonna try that much more often
and I spend most days making pictures or thinking about making pictures
or masturbating
or thinking about masturbating
and I dream too much and don't write enough
and I'm trying to find GOD everywhere
trying to figure out this thing He made called a man

and the television set tells me that it's bareknuckled bombing
and if I had a tank or was a movie star my penis would be huge I guess
cuz that's what they keep telling me
and that's what I want cuz that's what being a man means
or least that's what they keep telling me

my pops

takes care of us

he puts the garbage out twice a week
he drives forty-five minutes to water flowers
I'm sitting on the bus on Valentine's Day
when a seven-year-old boy carrying a book of Robin Hood
sits down next to me and asks me my name
"Anis."
"That's a nice name."
"Thank you what's yours?"
"Quentin.
Anis? Do you wanna read with me?"

so tell me what my fingers are writing
my fingers open like gates when I type
and the wind is swinging in the wake
motherfucker
I lift bridges with poems
and forests grow
in my mother's eyes
I am looking for GOD
Quentin
while this world says fuck you for trying
for this world hates your eyes Quentin
for they are simple and pure
and Quentin
this world hates your fingers
little like the stems of flowers
for not being able to pick up the things you have left behind
because you are still learning to do so
I don't drink fight or fuck but these days Quentin
it's only two out of those three that I don't do
and I've fallen in love six seven eight nine times Quentin so I don't want to want to
but I still do
and I want to find GOD
in the morning
and
in the tired hands of dusk
at the mouth of the river and down by its feet
but instead
I drive sixty
through residential streets
praying to hit children

so that they may stay forever angels
and forever full of night and light and red and crayons
and simple outstretched limbs trying to pick up way too much way too fast
forgetting what it means to be a person
in a world
where egos are measured with tabloids
where automobiles double for morals
where beliefs are like naps
you leave them behind when somebody touches you
and in a place where oil always takes precedence over life
I find myself sitting on a bus watching a small boy float down like fresh water
carrying a book I used to
asking if I want to share what he sees if only for a little while
and I do
and then asks if I want to give to him what I see if only for a little while
and I read to him
and then says to me he is going to show me the world
and starts reading me the words himself
moving his hands beneath the sentences
not noticing all the time what is written
sometimes skipping whole lines
because his fingers are moving faster then what they are showing his eyes
and I want to tell him slow
down Quentin

slow down

you don't have to touch and go
you can see it all if your finger whispers on one word

slow down Quentin
and hold what you see just a little bit longer
for you are already holding my attention
and in a world of fast faces
I'm looking for GOD everywhere
trying to figure out a little better
this little thing He made called a man ■

Bob Whoopeecat Stephenson

Finals Night—Five Needles (Part I)

Poet and SlamMaster from Dallas, Whoopeecat is also a member of the PSi Executive Council.

As a kid jumping from lofts into piles of hay in southern Alabama, I never realized the significance of the old adage, "that's like finding a needle in a haystack," until some thirty-five years later in August of 2005. Charged with being a bout manager for the National Poetry Slam Finals in Albuquerque, I was given the task to find five judges for the event that would be unbiased. A nice cross representation of the population if you will, and did I mention none could be residents of Albuquerque?

This task seemed to be overwhelming. Find five in hundreds who would not have a hometown bias toward a hometown team competing in the final. I shared my concerns with Taneka Stotts, member of the host city committee. She volunteered to help me find impartial judges, and we set a strategy. The best way to find needles, stick your hands in the stack and start feeling. We jumped in the crowd of audience members waiting in the lobby thirty minutes prior to doors opening. Methodical census interviews of hay strands ensued as we searched for unique little needles that would stick out and be noticed. Diligence pays off.

We had a variety of judges from the likes of Minnesota, Vermont, Oregon, and Iowa. A spectral range of skin tones, ages, and sexuality were represented. After presenting the judges to the contestants, one team felt a pair of ladies we had chosen was too close to the competition. They recognized them as judges from a preliminary bout, a point not mentioned when interviewed. Taneka and I quickly moved to a backup interviewee, a gentleman stationed on a military facility hailing from Maryland. He was quickly embraced by the contestants, and the five judges were set. ■

Bob Whoopeecat Stephenson
"Q"

Let's have a short conversation about . . . "Q"
Now I'm not talkin' about that obscure 17th letter in the alphabet
that begins a miniscule 312 words
and has more phonetic symbols
than any other letter to describe how it sounds
kinda' "Q,"

or the hardest key to reach on the keyboard
with your left pinky
without hitting the tab key
"Q,"

or that sexy little ten-point tile
that every Scrabble fiend loves to unleash
in a Double Letter/Triple Word Score
kinda' "Q,"

or that letter so tight
in its relationship with the vowel "U"
it covers his six as a backup partner
bustin' through the front door
of every word

Although some of the most beautiful words in language like:
quiver, quake, queer, quittance, quasar, quintet,
Quetzalcoatl (kèts'l kō áatl), Quixote, Québécois
and queen rule the "Q's"

You can try to quote me on this. . . .

but I sometimes must be quarantined
in a quantum quandary trying to qualify
queries in to the quintessential quixotic quiddity
of this quizzical . . . kind of "Q"!

So what kind of "Q" are we talkin' about?
It's the kind of "Q" that's going to leave you so hungry
by the time I finish this poem
you're going to wipe the drool from your lip
with your sleeve

and it's so popular in culinary culture
its name was shortened
to a one syllable word like a movie or rock star
"Q"

and it's served with sauce
SO DAMN GOOD!
it has to be basted and swabbed on with a mop
because paintbrushes around the grill and pit
are for PUSSIES!

Better yet,
it's SO DAMN GOOD
it doesn't even need sauce
kinda' "Q"!

It's sooooo tempting
it causes vegetarians, vegans,
chickitarians, pescatarians,
Catholics, Muslims and Jews
to question their convictions.

and it's sooooo enticing
you're going to tie your tongue so tight
around a rib bone
all you can moan is . . .
"mmmmmmm that's eggggXcellent "Q"!

and it can only be served
potluck style with
cheap beer, sweet tea,
homemade potato salad,
iron-skillet baked beans,

coleslaw, and fried pickles,
on a paper plate!
with a roll of Brawny paper towels
so you can wipe your face, hands
and tuck them into shirt for a bib
kinda "Q"!
and Moms tell Dads,
"Break out the homemade peach ice cream
in the hand crank maker"
'cause there's no better dessert
for this kinda "Q"

and better yet
Mom slaps the ever livin' shit out of you
because it's better than her
legendary "Q."

So are ya' hungry yet?

I know I am,
but before you go wasting money
betting on a "quinella" to pick the winners
of the next presidential election

Why don't you trust me . . .
pull up a seat . . .
join the quorum
no need to quell temptation
just quench your appetite
because there is no Quid Pro Quo
for this kind of "Q"! ▪

Dasha Kelly

Hosting the Event

Poet and organizer from Milwaukee, Wisconsin, Dasha Kelly is soon-to-be host and organizer of the 2008 Nationals in Madison, Wisconsin. She was also cohost of the team finals at NPS 2005.

I can usually grab a seat in one of the center sections. Not too close, and not so far back that theatre shadows will tickle my attention. Slam finals, for me, is always a gift. It's at least one night for us to smudge away boundaries of state lines,

Figure 20. Dasha Kelly Hosting Slam Finals at NPS 2005. *Courtesy of David Huang*

Slam tenure, and literary skill. As artists, we are "the masses" instead of the minority for a change. On this night, the poets rule the world, and I try to make sure I have a great seat.

In 2005, I was invited to experience Slam finals from a completely different vantage point: *from the stage*! Thankfully, I'm not a rookie emcee, nor am I nervous in front of crowds. Otherwise, I might have melted into the floor when I first walked out and smiled into an audience that was easily the size of a small rural town—more than 2,000 folks, and their excitement was palpable! Actually, the entire week in Albuquerque had been a five-star experience, so this finals night was destined to be one for the history books.

And I was right. The performance hall vibrated with great energy right through the final words. Even inside the rough tangle of some of those words, the night was fantastic. I was glad to have had the best seat in the house. ▪

Dasha Kelly

Home

I am a
People watcher
Observant of the curves, curls
Ticks, giggles, strolls
and intended devilment of
complete strangers
In the club
I peep the creep
Of last call lovers
Two shopping carts
From being next, I
watch
Rusty little boys
Pool their coins
For pockets of sweetness
On the streets, I
seek
faces passersby
so I can read the broken lines
of their handwritten epic poems
I can't help but wonder
About the lyrics
I wear on my own face
Wonder if people can read
My one-line poem of
Four, waterlogged words:
My son died today.

My
Son
He was four months
too young to

Sing
With angels
Or dance inside the circle
Of ancestors
And those four words
slice tick marks
into my tongue
Keeping track of
how many times
My soul
Could fall apart
And slap itself back together

My son died today.

Four words
I carried with me
to the gypsy lady
hoping she might read my palms
Instead, she plucked a folk song
On the lifelines
that stretched from my skin
Into my dreams
Caramel colored lines
Charting destiny in my palms
Tangling my left hand in the future
While my right hand stays tethered
to his past
Caramel colored lines
Holding me suspended
between everything
and nothing
Floating
Easy
like spider's silk

Caramel
colored
lines
upon which I also
sign
my name into a
lifetime membership
whose dues are burned into my flesh
burned into my flesh
a series of numbers and symbols
tapping reluctant good-byes
like Morse code
from my soul
straight to heaven

Two
Eighteen
dash
Six
Twenty-eight
Dash
Two thousand
Four
dash
I love you
Dash
I miss you
Dash
I wish
you could have stayed
Period.

I always thought
it would be a
bath

to usher me into grown-up-dom
a girlfriend once told me about
a gray pubic hair
that winked back at her
from behind jasmine-scented bubbles
So, I just knew
That a gray, curly pube
would be my permission
To start wearing big hats
Purple gowns and generously
Tossing around affections like
Honey, sweetie, dumplin' and
Shhhuuugahhhh
But
burying
your own child
Moves you to the front
of that grown-up line
In fact, puts you off
to the side
where you find
Silent members of this secret club
Dapping
each other with their eyes
Wearing uniform undergarments
Stitched in grief
And together
we hum harmonies
of a fight song
Whenever daydreams
Fracture
into that nightmare mosaic
And still, we keep dancing
Keep smiling
Keep loving

Keep praying
Keep believing
Not to let these tears be
shed in vain
We make our pledge to keep
living

And I make a pledge to keep
Those four words
Forever tucked beneath my tongue
Even though they make me
Dizzy
sometimes
That's when I focus
My blurred eyes
on my firstborn
My daughter
Who tells
anyone who listens
how her baby brother
Now lives in heaven
And that makes me smile
sometimes
So I remind myself that
I am a
people
watcher
So I recognize
Otherwise,
too
I recognize
that my son was
not of this place

He came
the same way he left:
an angel

So I smudge away
The lyrics
Of my one-line poem
And change it so it reads:
My son did not die today
He just
went
Home ■

Aaron Cuffee
Pink and Brown
Team Albuquerque

My father
Used to tell me a story about when I was little
He said
That I could never understand the concept of
Black and White
That I used to refer to everyone as either
Pink or Brown

And you could only be a different shade of those colors
I was luckily spared the pain of racism most of my life,
But I hear about a time when
Returning from a trip to Florida
I got lost in the airport
And
My father
At the brink of a heart attack goes to look for me
When suddenly over the PA system
There was the distant call of

"We have a lost child at the American Airlines ticket counter,
Responds to the name Aaron, would his parents please
Come and get him"

Frantic father standing at the counter saying
"I think you have my son?"

" . . . Are you sure sir?"

"Yes!! My son Aaron!"
          "Well, we have a child here, but I don't think
                    he's yours."

Six foot tall nigger comin' at the frail moron at the counter
With all three hundred pounds behind him

"Listen bitch, I don't care what you think, but you better get my son out here right now or I'll
break you goddamnedlegs!"

That's my pop
But the bitch has big balls of steel
Leans into his ear and says

      "Listen to me boy . . . stay away from our kids."
Takes all the strength he has to keep from giving her head to me as a toy
Goes and gets Mom
Who, it just so happens, is of a more acceptable pigment

Leave the airport
But I couldn't understand why Dad was hugging me so tight
And why he couldn't stop crying

What's wrong Dad

What's wrong Dad

Grow up
And move to Irish/Italian mob movie
Set in a middle school

When one kid stands up in the cafeteria and yells

"Hey, porch monkey! Yeah, I'm talking to you jungle boy, c'mere and lick my boot."

Six feet tall in seventh grade, two hundred pounds, and mad at the whole fucking world
You do not
Wanna mess with me

On meatloaf Wednesday

I walk over tray in hand, and grin the size of the Grand Canyon on my face

"Were you talking to me?"

"Oh, lookit that, the mute nigger lover, it speaks now but it must be retarded. I told you
to lick my boot . . ."

Hours later
Crying on my bed
Cuz I can't understand why the kid
Whose ribs I broke
Is getting so much attention
And I get suspended

It's okay though
Cuz now people get out of my way in the halls
And when they say nigger
They look at me and apologize
So now, you've got the most dangerous weapon society can produce
A person who doesn't care anymore

235 fights in three years
32 kids hospitalized
40 suspensions
And one stab wound in woodshop
That left me with a scratch on the love handles, and the other kid
In traction

But I lost my desire to get in trouble
Dad telling me
"One fight in high school and they will kick you out, no jokes this time!"

But every time I see a face that wants to start shit,
I remember the people who would ask if I was "OK"

Whenever my father held my hand in the store
Or the ladies who'd cling their purses tighter whenever we walked by

I love my Mom
And I love my Dad
And I've always wanted to be just like him

Even though I know I can't

So, now all I want is some respect

Because my mother is not a whore
And my father's not a boy, he's a man
And I, I am not half anything
I am crawling along the most underground of railroads, across the biggest border in the
    world
The border of people's perceptions

Because I will never be
A nigger or a honky
A jiggaboo or whitebread
I'm not a spearchucker, a half-breed, an oreo, or a zebra
I'm not a wigger, a wannabe, or tainted meat

I am Aaron Cuffee
And I love

I love pink
And
I love brown ▪

Hakim Bellamy and Carlos Contreras
Rebel Music
Team Albuquerque

if I ruled the world
I'd free all my sons
black diamonds and pearls
if I ruled the world

if I ruled the world
I'd touch all
coldhearted politicians
with the heat from the beats of djs
and pen peace to release these
heat waves

he waves
as if Mr. America's real lies
and Ms. America's fake smiles
may save us
from the unintentional tension
that creates a hate crime
and hate crimes
we do

modern day minorities
hate the hate crime
but at the same time
hate the fact that if
it ain't a hate crime
eyes of justice turn to the
hated
let me re-state it

like what he's saying is
plainly stated
in every history book
with their withholding information
and whitewashed framing

me and my kind are the hated
you only love us
when we're entertaining
so we open mouths
to expose souls
modern day minstrels
playing to sold-out shows
spitting these poems
to sold-out souls

My fuckin' brother is on a roll . . .
and this time we can't
be put on hold

please hold
all our lines
are tied up
stay on the line
stay on the line
stay on the line

cuz we're like
customer service
serving you
line for line
and
word for wording
you
like
prophetic preachers
and three minute
ministers

see our brothers
and sisters
our words get
twisted and sinister
cuz

we're on a motherfuckin'
roll like rock
like pop
hip hop
and to the . . .

hip hop
the hibbie
to the hip hip
hopa you don't
stop a rockin' to the
bang bang
boogie said up
jump the boogie
of the rhythm of the boogie
to beat. . . .

hop sweatshops in a single bound
knock down Nike and Wal-Mart corporate headquarters
bordering Borders buildings down, downtown
bordering borders I now . . .

knot Nikes and walk smart past warlord death supporters
boarding up barriers
so the freed up memory in this mind state
allows us to vibrate
at phenomenal levels

spirit elevation
the advent of teleportation
may get us from this head space
to a better place

like mental verbal mind melding
"EXODUS, movement of Jah people"

from Latino to Negro
from knee-high to a million fists deep
raise them rather than throw them
because we've already begun to tell now show them
where the preexisting fractures are

from history book misprints
to neck to noose imprints
we're beaten by the way our skin tints or
better shades of reality

"Hi, my name is . . . !"
Slim
6'3
high blood pressure from the pressure of being a blood
crippled from being poverty-stricken
most of us already in prison, but don't worry, I'm on my way

dreadfully locked and brown-eyed
the suspect is a black male, 6'3, possibly armed and dangerous . . .
and I am suspect
susceptible to ghetto tales
in which we rebel yell,
"Iya. . . . Rebel Music"

as we move forward, through corrective lenses
not back to see what happened like forensics
really looking forward
not like clairvoyant pretenders
"call me nahhh . . ."
called four eyes for looking through black-and-white lenses
'cause we can't see colors

but time and space give my third eye
a third dimension
as we look through 3-D lenses or
better shades of reality

"a rebel music . . . !"

Stephen Sargent
They Love You Not
Performed by Stephen Sargent and K. A. Williams for Team Ft. Worth.

They love how your skin comes in honey, caramel chocolate and cocoa brown
    complexions,
so they sunbathe, trying to gain your tone's perfection
They love u they love u not.
They love the thickness of your lips and the curves of the hips you in
so they try to replicate by injecting collagen.
They love you they love you not!
They love the versatility of your crown,
how you look good whether it's fro-ed out, cut or just laying down
like black men who laid their lives down from Crispus Attucks to World War II vets
who fought Hitler and came home to face Jim Crow.
We give our respects to freedom fighters who saved this country's life,
but America forgot!
They love u they love u not!
They love you.
They love you not!
They love soouuuL food! From fried chicken, collard greens, corn bread, sweet potato
pie and black-eyed peas!
And hot sauce?
Man, they love hot sauce!
And red Kool-Aid too!
And Brown sugar!
They want some of your Brown sugar!
But they won't tell you!
They love your music, from hip hop, soul, gospel and R&B,
that's why they gave you shout-outs on they last CD.
Why, I had this one dude tell me he was blacker than me and said
I didn't know enough about hip hop 'cause I hadn't copped the new Fitty Cent CD,
rolling down the street thinking that music makes you understand how our live be!
But when the Five O shows up it's ALL EYEZ ON ME!
They love u they love u not.

They love that smooth way you speak.

They trying to talk like every word you said.

They even love Martin and Malcolm after they dead.

When? After they dead!

HOW? After they dead!

They love Denzel, Colin Powell, and Maya Angelou.

Why, they favorite thing to do is to watch the Oprah show.

And you get a car!

And you get a car!

And you get a car!

They love you.

They love you not!

They love your music, your style, your churches, your soul,

Your features, your tones, they love the way you party, the way you preach,

the way you praise, the way you raise the roof.

Just examine you life, they can't deny the charges!

You can't deny the charges! We're living proof of the charges!

Don't believe the hype. They may love you today!

Then hate you tonight! Sing Hosanna.

Then Crucify the Christ! Live in America. That's just a nigga's plight.

I never understood the slaughter, then studied history and realized that oppression

was jealousy's daughter,

so that which is original will always be hated.

And martyrdom will always be the price to pay for greatness!

And they will always love our style, our words, our tones, our walk, our life

but they don't love us! ▪

CP Maze Forever and Q
Mirror, Mirror
Team Charlotte

Mirror, mirror on the wall
tell what dreams may come to prevent thy downfall
Mirror, mirror on the wall
tell what dreams may come to prevent thy downfall
Mirror, mirror on the wall
tell what dreams may come to prevent thy downfall

Most backsliding in present ways
lost through present days,
if we don't work,
we don't eat.
If we don't run,
our dreams don't shine.
Tomorrow is an ever eluding illusion.
Tomorrow is nothing more than a bastard born crying,
hoping that we cradle him in these hands of time,
so tomorrow we must live life like we just might die.
Tomorrow is not promised.
We know not why this is the only promised dream's forget.
Today is here.
Take advantage before your motivation splits,
begins a nine to five, working overtime,
and over time the will will have gone away,
and there won't be no way except for these instructions left in your will.
Will you sign on the dotted line to keep your dreams alive?
I'll donate a pint of poems
to save a life
'cause I'm feeling like the uni–Jeger bomber.
Osama been writing poems in caves,
sending packages in the U.S. postal maze.
Cash on delivery, accept them with opening this lyrical phrase.
Can I get my money back if this shit don't explode in my face?
Take me at face value, but don't erase these lines
A crows' feet will drop from the sky and pluck out the wisdom in your eyes,

eyes wide shut like perfect Sunday Christians on Thursday,
twisting up trees while brothers are still pack head bouncing
from boy scout knots on branches
we hold limbs in our lips and break bread with our thoughts,
turn time into wine to get the party started.
There's a man in the mirror
and the roof of my mouth
and he's playing a concrete violin.
I'm asking him to change his ways.
No question should have been asked any clearer
If you want to make the world a better place,
take a look at yourself and make a change,
'cause right now things are going bad,
and I'd rather ask me instead of you.
I'm off the wall,
avoiding reflections mirroring M.C. Escher's re-re-re-remix.
Mirror mirror on the wall
mirror mirror on the wall
mirror mirror on the wall
are you ready for your dreams to come true?
Do you claim your life as an experience
or as an experiment?
It's amazing how beakers become shot glasses
and butts and burners breathe like lighters underneath weed bowls.
We bowl beauty backwards until she chokes back words and strike out life.
Yeah, motherfucker,
that's what I'm talking about.
I'm talking about these dreams I daydream at night
from the mirror
no reflection
all in the moonlight
with the maze full of metaphors
all on cue
all on you.
Mirror, mirror on the wall,
tell what dreams may come to prevent thine downfall. ■

Javon Johnson

Dance

Team Hollywood

If I had twenty-four hours to live
If I had twenty-four hours to live
I'd dance
Like some four-year-old girl who's off beat
But happy because everyone around her is smiling
I'd dance
Like some fifteen-year-old boy who's listening to music for the first time in his life
I'd dance
For no good goddamned reason at all
I'd dance
Like the zebra and the gazelle in *The Lion King*
Who danced to that song
"Circle of Life"
For this little baby lion who will someday grow large enough and eat them
But regardless they danced
So I too will dance
Thickheaded
Chest stuck out
Swelled with pride
Like I live inside of a music box
Ooh . . . but see that's the funny thing about boxes
They label
Then categorize
And once they categorize
You can only live according to definition they assign you
Well I refuse to live in a defined world so right now I say do what you want to do
Right now I say dance
Dance because some White lady told me Black folks only go to college for sports
Dance because there are millions of kids
Who slow dance with death due to hunger
That wraps around their bellies like well-dressed earthquakes
Dance because there are another million kids
Who refuse to live in society's defined lines
So they color the world in hot pinks

Electric blues
Neon greens
And hot bright oranges
Dance because she said
Javon you're not really a poet
I mean you don't really write poetry
Well Picasso was never an artist
And Cubism was never art
Thelonious Monk was never a jazz musician
And Jazz was never music
And six years ago slam wasn't considered poetry
And at one point or another Black folks in this country wasn't even considered people
But regardless they danced in the middle of the night
To escape the daymares named slavery
So I too will dance
Dance like I'm going to live forever
Dance like I'm going to die tomorrow
Dance like I believe in reincarnation
Dance because you never heard a song quite like this one
Dance because this is your fucking song
Dance because contrary to popular belief
Dance because you hate popular belief
Some White guys do have rhythm
Dance because I said so
Dance because you want to
Dance because you don't
Just dance
Dance
Dance
Dance
Dance
So no
I will never be a poet by your definitions because my words
Dance ■

Bob Whoopeecat Stephenson

Finals Night—Five Needles (Part II)

During finals, I was a bout manager with Phil West backstage. My stage-left perspective made for a good vantage point to see poems from the wings and monitor the entry and exit of poets from the mic. Javon Johnson and Crystal Irby, Team Hollywood, delivered a blistering duet of the "emergency negro cast system" to lead off the evening. Charlotte gave a taste of incredible teamwork that would be the focal point of their evening. Ft. Worth, fresh off a Janean Livingston dramatic slam-off for a tied title in the individual competition, swept up onstage with another strong group piece. The hometown team from Albuquerque followed with a racial parody team piece. The first seven poems of the evening embraced strong group unity. Then Rives, of Hollywood, shifted gears. He delivered banter and repartee that included catch phrases, slogans, and musical interludes from pop culture to commercials. He worked memorable lines from poets' performing moments before his time in the spotlight and proved with a Tourette's tick that "he is the best listener." This shift to solo performances carried on with Janean Livingston (Ft. Worth), Cuffee (Albuquerque), and Javon Johnson (Hollywood).

I was keeping score backstage and noted all the teams were still able to win nearing the final round. Charlotte stuck to their plan of group pieces and delivered a phenomenal duet with Maze Forever and Q in a wonderfully choreographed piece playing social mirror images against and with each other. The energy was back to team pieces for the rest of the performance. As we came to the last poem of the evening, it was apparent that no one could catch the hometown team from Albuquerque. Reserved and professional in their exuberance, the team hugged each other and patiently waited for their next moment onstage.

Energy buzzed through the auditorium as the last poem was complete. I took a seat in the front row with friends to view the presentation. As the emcees called the teams to the stage, I noticed a cloud of disappointment building. It grew in intensity and number of poets onstage and struck the crowd with a flash of crossed arms and thunderous protest as the awards were being handed out. I quickly moved to the stairs stage right as an altercation between Danny Solis, Artistic Director, and poets from the competition flared. The altercation moved backstage, and I stood sentinel between Esmé Vaandrager on the microphone and the roaring voices in the wings. As tempers calmed and the show came to a close with a statement from Danny, poets, audience, and organizers left puzzled at the outcome.

Accusations of misconduct and improper behavior in one night would leave a blemish on an entire week of entertainment and poetry that proved to be one of the most memorable in National Poetry Slam history. Judges were consistent and executed their duties with integrity. Poets backstage during the competition were respectful of other competitors on the mic. In the end the hometown team prevailed. Success had nothing to do with odds stacked in their favor. It emerged from their poetic ability to capture the hearts and minds of the audience and five unique needles found in a stack. ▪

Figure 21. Bob Whoopeecat Stephenson. *Courtesy of Sarah Ausherman*

Editors

Finals Controversy

A small group of teams started complaining when the Albuquerque organizers changed the semifinals venue. There seemed to be some feeling that the host city was trying to create an advantage for Team Albuquerque by putting them in a venue farthest from downtown that would hold a huge (hometown) audience but would be harder for out-of-towners to get to. It was completely chance that Team Albuquerque's semifinal ended up at the National Hispanic Cultural Center, but the teams who questioned it didn't care.

On finals night, two of the competing teams believed they heard booing from the audience and even from backstage. The hometown team was thought to have too much support from the hometown audience.

The performances were stellar from all the teams, and the competition stayed tight through the final round. When the winner was declared and Albuquerque went to claim their trophy, two of the teams stood with arms crossed into Xs, while Queen Sheba of Charlotte acted as spokesperson to express the teams' distress.

The youngest member of Team Albuquerque, Esmé Vaandrager, who had not been able to compete because she was too young, took the mic to perform her only poem of the four-day event. The protest continued behind her, with things heating up. For Team Albuquerque, this disrespect to poetry and to their young teammate was unbelievable. For those protesting Team Albuquerque's win, reading an additional poem seemed like a victory lap, as it was not customary at finals and not immediately understood. With all the hubbub, the explanation was lost.

Danny went onstage to support the cohosts, Karen Finneyfrock and Dasha Kelly, and to clear the stage. There were intimations of violence backstage between Danny and Hollywood team member Javon before things finally settled down.

The Executive Council of PSi later asked for firsthand accounts from all involved and other witnesses in the audience and backstage. Ultimately, it found the other teams' claims to be unsubstantiated, and it handed out punishments to many involved based on the Code of Honor that all poets sign to participate in the event. Some protesting team members later apologized for the way it all played out. In the end, the sound and fury died down, and Albuquerque was still hometown of that year's Team Champions and the host city for a Nationals boat so big that even controversy couldn't upset it. ■

Mike Henry

The Event and the Controversy

Poet and SlamMaster from Austin, Mike Henry organized his third Nationals in Austin in 2007 and was bout manager at finals during NPS 2005.

When Dickens wrote, "it was the best of times, it was the worst of times," it seems unlikely he was intending to pen prophesy about the National Poetry Slam. But sure enough, I have a clear memory of that sentence coming into my head as I stood in a small but swelling sea of poets screaming at one another backstage at the 2005 NPS finals.

It had been a truly spectacular week. Since my baptism into the National Poetry Slam in 1995, I haven't missed one—and don't ever intend to—and the week in Albuquerque was the best I'd ever seen. As someone who has been on the organizing side of NPS many times, I think it's difficult for most people to fully appreciate the scope of the event, the mammoth challenge that it has evolved into. 'Burque rose up, embraced our family like they'd been waiting for us our whole lives, and we had a hell of a great week.

Then, finals night came. I was one of the bout managers working backstage on Saturday night when the top teams and individual competitors came to rock it. Great theater, great performances, great show . . . until the very end of the night. As the winning team—which just happened to be the home team from Albuquerque—took the stage to receive their trophy, members of some of the opposing teams chose to stand onstage with their arms raised above their heads in X shapes to protest. They had their reasons. I'm not here to argue that, whether I agree with those reasons or not.

Onstage, it was one of those moments when time slowed down. The idyllic week I'd experienced imploded into chaos: poets bumrushing the mic to get their last word in, bout officials trying to clear the stage of protesting poets, while a young woman from the Albuquerque Team tried to give one more poem to the audience. The scene backstage suddenly became more Jerry Springer than arts event. It wouldn't be fair or useful to go further into it than that.

I will say this; from my perspective, there was no question who won the team bout that night. All the teams were great, which is usually the case at finals. One team took it, earned it, and owned it, straight up. That team just happened to be the home team.

The winning and the losing as part of the DNA of Slam is a built-in testing ground, an internal minefield for all of us. There have been lots of beefs and arguments over the years about what happened (or didn't happen) at Nationals. Sometimes these discussions occur in meetings of rules committees that play into the wee hours in some hotel room somewhere. Most of the time, they just get hashed over at the bar after the show. But at the root of almost every disagreement, you will find the question of winning and losing. Anyone who says different is selling something. As a slammer, you work and scrap for years on your home stage and pack all that baggage into brief moments in the sun at Nationals. And usually, you lose. How do you deal with that? That's the interesting stuff to me.

Here's the thing: I've always told poets in my scene that Slam will teach you as much about how to live as it does how to write and perform. It is a highly charged, unpredictable world populated by people who, by definition, have a lot of strongly held opinions, are not afraid to express them, and are damn good at it. I think if you watch closely at slams, you'll find out as much about the poets by watching the choices they make as you do by listening to the stories they rip on the mic. Who is driven by competition? Who is about the community? Who is motivated by personal gratification? How each of us chooses to walk in this world of Slam is more important than what poem you read in the first round or the scores given by any judge. The fact that a structure exists that puts such valuable windmills for us to joust at in terms of our personal journeys, plus is the best stone by which to sharpen our poetic craft, plus puts enough butts in the seats that any of this matters at all, is true testament to the vision that Marc Smith had when he created the game. It is not surprising that many of us have dedicated significant parts of our lives to its service.

I learned a lot that night. Some poets and promoters that I'd known and respected for years morphed before my eyes into nothing more than thugs—loudmouthed and selfish. Some words got said that can't be taken back. I think the audience suffered for it, which is antithetical to what this whole thing is supposed to be about.

We grow from what we experience in Slam, and we often have to heal from it, too. In the end, some individuals rose above it all and saved my soul that night in Albuquerque, which is just the sort of thing that happens at Slam from time to time. ■

Mike Henry
Marriage

The plant that hangs over the sink needs some attention.

Overgrown, surrounding itself and sneaking in a slow twist,
it is strangling, a hundred small wrists against necks. Steam from
dishwashing, scrubbing vegetables, water glasses emptied before
bed. We remember to water it, too often.

Months ago, it was a cascade of small heart-shaped leaves,
a wave suspended above the water. Now, it could be a bird's nest.
My grandmother's hairdo, the day before she remembers the salon.

After some debate it is decided that we must untangle, create a new start.
It's the hearts, see, that's our favorite shape, well, hers really, but mine
because of and so, it begins.

I notice out loud how it is a knot, a pile of wet spaghetti, a macramé owl.
I comment about how we are knitting a sweater backwards.
Apparently, this is neither as helpful or as funny as I would have hoped.

We are pulling through and back and over, around and handing the
fragile strands that cry gentle, snapping at the slightest snag.
This life is tenuous, and I am clumsy, at best.

I feel a slow crescendo of strain in my stiffening back, bent over, studying
this small chaos, hoping for a clue. She sits cross-legged, like yoga.
I seem to be bigger and less flexible. A drop of my sweat splashes the floor.
I wonder if she thinks it's gross.

I swallow grins as she cusses at every lost heart, spitting sharp shits
with t's punctuating the air as another strand goes down for the cause,
swept to the pile.

We get frustrated somewhere between the first and second act, our sentences
deconstructing into fragmented bursts of Don't and No and but I was . . .
She tries to let me off the hook, but I won't take it. She offers to do it herself.
Where's the fun in that, I say.

There are minutes of only breathing, in which I, of course, find myself thinking
about sex. I shift focus, squint through the maze of tendrils for a glimpse of her,
the narcotic swoop of her hipbone.

Ill-advisedly, I suggest somewhere in the middle that we're never going to get there,
and conversation turns philosophical. There are ramifications to the
fêng shui, and the kitchen is the marriage corner of the house.

Eventually a system weaves itself into being, her small fingers untangling
while I just stick my arms out, like what could be branches holding the freed vines
out at angles akin to shattered glass. Hand the vine from hers to mine, unweaving
     the net,
over and under, one pushing, one pulling, this deliberate dance of hands.

The clock on the stove counts hours.
At some point I notice we're both smiling, punch-drunk and
unable to make coherent sentences. Hungry, she laughs.

And in the end, we've done it and a dozen mostly bare green strands spread
out like a picture of the sun fingerpainted by a child, lines jagged and random,
but sweet. Maybe it is long wet hair, spread after a shower.

And as the sunlight fades to dusk in Texas, it's like I'm in a cartoon,
looking down at the world's sincerest Christmas tree, the bare, brave branches
gesturing out against an imaginary wind that makes apologies to the dusting of
green needles that scatter the snow, and I grin a little and look up at her,
and her eye glints with mischief, and before I can open my mouth she says,
Merry Christmas, Charlie Brown.

And if that isn't true love, then I don't know what is. ▪

Taylor Mali

Best-Run National Poetry Slam

Monday, May 28, 2007

For reasons both personal and political, poetic and prosaic, or, to speak more plainly, *for reasons both good and bad*, I will always remember the 2005 National Poetry Slam in Albuquerque. It was one of the best-run nationals ever—perhaps even the single best—despite the drama of what happened at the finals, and despite the butting of heads that always seems to happen when strong personalities with strong opinions clash. But I'm getting ahead of myself.

Albuquerque in 2005 was looking like it would be my last National Poetry Slam as a competitor. Unless my team won again—in which case I would take my customary year off and try to come back and win again in 2007 (for the sixth time!)—Albuquerque would be the end of the road for me as a slammer. I wanted to go down swinging. No longer president of PSi, and with the debacle of the 2004 NPS in St. Louis fast becoming a distant and calamitously humorous memory, I was excited to just focus on trying to win and have fun.

And in terms of fun, the hospitality of Hotel Blue almost provided enough to make the week complete without any poetry whatsoever. You couldn't have designed a better place for poets to hang out, rest, party, or (on a few occasions) run around naked. So accommodating, so relaxed, so trusting. No one was surprised when the management of the hotel and the building itself won the coveted Spirit of the Slam award on Saturday night.

The event itself seemed flawless, and that was due in large part to the vision of the host city director, Danny Solis, and the team of dedicated and intelligent people whose arms he no doubt had twisted into helping him. Everything from the graphic design to the venues to the parties indicated that forethought and experience had been in abundance during the planning stages. Solis and I have not always seen eye to eye. I have not always respected him, nor has he, me. But he did it up right in his hometown that year. And often it has been the case that a strong-headed director almost single-handedly makes a National Poetry Slam a success. That was the case with Ray Davey in Providence in 2000 and Marc Smith in 2003. Other years, the success seems driven by the director's sublime ability to envelope the community with a spirit of cooperation: think Allan Wolf in Asheville in 1994 or Cynthia French in Minneapolis in 2002.

But on the night of the finals, controversy erupted when a member of the second-place finishing Charlotte team inappropriately reprimanded the entire audience for bad behavior. Apparently, from backstage it seemed as if there had been more than your average amount of booing (there's always a fair amount of booing at a slam, but I don't remember it being out of hand). Of course, Albuquerque won the slam that night, the only other time that the host city has ever won the National Poetry Slam since Boston in 1992 (usually home teams don't even make it to the finals!). The home field advantage was just too much for any of the other teams to overcome.

I know I am writing this account for a book about the Albuquerque Slam scene culminating in the wonderful National Poetry Slam that they hosted, and to say what I'm about to say might make me unpopular, but to be totally honest—a phrase I rarely use because I am always honest—Charlotte was the better team and really *should* have won that night. In fact, I would even go so far as to say Ft. Worth deserved second place (believe it or not, I really *would* like to be welcome back in Albuquerque sometime). I think the five judges chosen at random from the audience—not all from Albuquerque, it must be said—were just too easily swayed by the overwhelmingly New Mexican crowd, which was rightfully ecstatic at seeing their local, but relatively inexperienced team, competing in the finals. In my opinion, Albuquerque should have tied for third with the team from Hollywood, which actually came in fourth.

In New York, we have a saying about poetry slams: "The best poet always loses." I think a similar statement could be said about the National Poetry Slam every year: "The best team never wins." If that's the worst thing I can say about the National Poetry Slam of 2005, then I don't find it contradictory at all to maintain *at the same time* that it may well have been the best nationals ever. ▪

Taylor Mali
What Teachers Make

or
Objection Overruled
or
If things don't work out, you can always go to law school

He says the problem with teachers is, "What's a kid going to learn
from someone who decided his best option in life was to become a teacher?"
He reminds the other dinner guests that it's true what they say about
teachers:
Those who can, do; those who can't, teach.

I decide to bite my tongue instead of his
and resist the temptation to remind the other dinner guests
that it's also true what they say about lawyers.

Because we're eating, after all, and this is polite company.

"I mean, you're a teacher, Taylor," he says.
"Be honest. What do you make?"

And I wish he hadn't done that
(asked me to be honest)
because, you see, I have a policy
about honesty and ass-kicking:
if you ask for it, I have to let you have it.

You want to know what I make?

I make kids work harder than they ever thought they could.
I can make a C+ feel like a Congressional Medal of Honor
and an A- feel like a slap in the face.
How dare you waste my time with anything less than your very best.

I make kids sit through forty minutes of study hall
in absolute silence. No, you may not work in groups.
No, you may not ask a question.
Why won't I let you get a drink of water?
Because you're not thirsty, you're bored, that's why.

I make parents tremble in fear when I call home:
I hope I haven't called at a bad time,
I just wanted to talk to you about something Billy said today.
Billy said, "Leave the kid alone. I still cry sometimes, don't you?"
And it was the noblest act of courage I have ever seen.

I make parents see their children for who they are
and what they can be.

You want to know what I make?

I make kids wonder,
I make them question.
I make them criticize.
I make them apologize and mean it.
I make them write, write, write.
And then I make them read.
I make them spell definitely beautiful, definitely beautiful, definitely
beautiful
over and over and over again until they will never misspell
either one of those words again.
I make them show all their work in math.
And hide it on their final drafts in English.
I make them understand that if you got this (brains)
then you follow this (heart) and if someone ever tries to judge you
by what you make, you give them this (the finger).

Let me break it down for you, so you know what I say is true:
I make a goddamn difference! What about you?

Esmé Vaandrager

The Team

Dancer, artist, filmmaker, and poet, Esmé Vaandrager was the youngest member of an Albuquerque Slam Team for two years in a row.

I think 2005 was the year I really had my "Welcome to the Family" artistic experience. Albuquerque's poetry scene had already been very congenial when I was introduced as a fourteen-year-old poet, shaking at the mic. That summer, though, I got to walk among giants, and then stood alongside them at the end as they collected their prize.

So, to introduce "the boys," as I lovingly refer to the talented, caring men I was lucky enough to call teammates:

- It always gave me a scare when I saw Carlos's name on slam sign-ups.
- Cuffee was a powerhouse who could get louder better than anyone I'd seen.
- Hakim had been winning often with his fast and pertinent attacks and informed writing.
- Kenn was the only coach I'd had, and a wise, experienced figure in the Slam community.
- I was the little sister. They all made me feel a part of the team, despite being too young to compete at our final goal—Nationals. I cannot thank them enough for that sense of belonging.

As soon as the team was chosen, we met to arrange rehearsals and begin writing. Our group pieces were special that year. We cut, pasted, and rearranged what we had each written on group prompts into new three-minute poems. After writing, we blocked and rehearsed almost every morning that summer. It helped that the team got along tremendously. The sense of family and solidarity was a comfort that poets who've been on slam teams will tell you is rare, precious, and vital to the enjoyment and efficacy of a team's artistic work together.

Other members of the community stopped in to check our progress. Danny Solis made us jump around Harwood's yard like animals. For the most part, though, we did not worry about outside input. "Kenn always believed in us!" recalls Carlos. In turn, we all trusted Kenn's poetic direction and strategic calls to the fullest. Our travels also strengthened the group bond. Despite the squeeze in the backseat, there was always much laughter, jokes in strange accents, and constant quotes from *Coming to America* and *Half Baked*. "Yes, Cuban B!"

As August approached, I spent more time observing with the stopwatch. At that point in the game, the boys could easily have pushed me to the sidelines to focus on group pieces for competition. Instead, they valued my input, and I learned tons from being allowed "in the incubator" with them. I only heard of the fun and crazy antics that filled the Hotel Blue while it was taken over by poets. I was busy skipping class to be at rehearsals—my stomach jumping right along with the boys' because even though I wasn't going to be onstage, I was part of the team, too, and had put in the time, work, and love to light it up for Nationals.

One of the most telling lessons I learned from the experience was at a high school performance the Monday after competition. Kenn announced that everyone was about to see some National Champions in Slam Poetry. Woo hoo. We could have won the neighborhood pet show. Only some explosive words were going to move the 8:00 a.m. haze in that auditorium.

In the end, I will value the friendships I made that summer for life. I pushed myself to improve my craft and come to a fuller understanding of myself as an artist and friend. That is a journey that takes something more than scores to mark the progress of. ∎

Kenn Rodriguez

Winning It All—Team ABQ 2005

At the time it seemed like a dream. Winning a National Poetry Slam title in your hometown—it doesn't happen. But it happened to Albuquerque. *In* Albuquerque.

Our team—Hakim Bellamy, Carlos Contreras, Cuffee, myself, and Esmé Vaandrager—were not the best poets. But hey, like Marc (So What!) Smith so famously said, "the best poet always loses" in Slam.

What we were was a team. We entered the competition as a team—a team that went beyond the five of us. Every ABQ poet who was at the opening ceremony hit the stage with us in front of Hotel Blue in Downtown ABQ. There were so many of us that we nearly broke the stage.

We finished with all four poets of the team onstage, with Esmé—who was too young to compete—standing in the wings. We hit the final words of that group poem and walked off, arms around each other, not giving a damn about the scores that came back because we knew we'd hit that poem, "We Teach," with as much *ganas* as we could muster.

And we left as a team, representing a community. I can say that no other team on the finals stage was so fully reppin' their town as Team ABQ was.

There were allegations that the books had been cooked, that we somehow didn't deserve the title. If someone was pulling strings, they never told us. We just went out and did our poetry—just like we did all summer.

No Poetry Slam team comes together at Nationals. If your team hasn't gelled by then, you're not going to do very well. Team ABQ came together long before NPS started in early August. Team ABQ gelled during 8:00 a.m. practices, three or four times a week at first.

On first look, the team might not have worked. Carlos and Hakim came from an R&B/hip hop influence. Very song based. Lots of wordplay—sweet-sounding rhymes and alliteration. Cuffee and I were both more free verse. But we were all more or less storytellers.

Team ABQ basically bonded over group poems. A lot of teams do group pieces out of some weird sense of duty—because that's what winning teams do. But they don't really enjoy the process.

Team ABQ used group poems to gel and to bond and to find common ground. That's what the team experience was all about—finding that common ground and amplifying it. It made us greater than the sum of our parts. None of us was gunning for a National Individual title. None of us was using the team as an audition for Def Poetry. We were completely team oriented. That immediately put us ahead of the pack.

We had seen something similar from Team Denver in 2004. They were a unit. They didn't fight. They were completely simpatico—in sync with each other in a way few teams ever are. We learned from watching our sister city's poets. We emulated them in a lot of ways. We also emulated past ABQ teams, past Austin teams—our other sister Slam city.

Again, no team gels at NPS. Team ABQ started getting it together in Austin at the Southwest Shootout. We lost to Austin, but we knew we had something going on with the work we were doing. Next we went to Big Sur, California, for the Western Regional. This time we pulled out a win going against poets from probably the most competitive poetry community in the country—the San Francisco Bay Area. Again, the road trip—and the camping we did at Big Sur—got us to gel as friends as well as poets. We spent four hours waiting at a car rental place in Los Angeles. Hakim slept. The rest of us just chilled and talked. A lot of teams might've had a meltdown. We just talked.

One final regional at Flagstaff showed us we were set. The other thing that showed us we were set: we practiced seventeen days straight after Big Sur—without even realizing we'd done it. We just got together everyday at 8:00 a.m. like clockwork and worked on our poems and performance. We knew we were entering the competition more prepared than anyone else.

Night one in the Golden West Saloon was a huge challenge. Going up against three teams is hard, but knowing we had a New York Team, Louder Arts (also known as Bar 13), made us edgy. We didn't perform with the confidence we'd had in the regionals, but we still placed second, putting us in a good situation. We didn't make the decisions based entirely on poetry. The whole summer we'd gone with what felt right. We forced some decisions on night one. That would be the last time.

Night two we were in the El Rey Theater. It was a bigger venue with a bigger, pro-ABQ crowd than the first evening. We were going against Houston and Los Angeles-Green among the teams. But something clicked. We just went with it. All summer long, we'd been practicing in just T-shirts and jeans. I'd been practicing barefoot. Night two, I skipped getting all dressed up and went rolled how I had all summer. We all did. And it showed. I forgot the beginning of my signature poem "I Am," and we still got it done. The group poems were spot on. Houston protested about Hakim changing shirts, but their protest wasn't well founded. We won on the stage.

That left us with a rematch against Bar 13 in the semifinals. We had early practice. Bar 13's coach was busy protesting that our bout would be at the National Hispanic Cultural Center—far from downtown and the host motel. We practiced. That was probably the difference. No one else in the semifinal with us thought they could beat Bar 13. But we almost had on Wednesday night and weren't performing at

100 percent. And they were distracted by nonpoetry issues. We'd just been living poetry.

That night again, we came out and just put the shine on it. Bar 13 kept close, but team thinking got us past it all. We knew we'd won before the final score was announced. We'd made finals.

Waking up Saturday, in my own bed, thinking that I was in the finals was a surreal experience. Almost every day, all summer I'd woken up around 7:30 and gotten going for practice. Saturday, despite staying up 'til 3:00 a.m. or so, I woke up at 7:30 as usual. We got together later and rolled to Carlos's apartment to practice. Halfway through, we botched a line in a group poem and just broke up laughing. Logan Phillips from Flagstaff and his girlfriend were in the room watching.

"That's why you're going to win," he said, "because you still enjoy each other's company."

Being superstitious, we just laughed it off. But it felt right. We were first to Kiva Auditorium that afternoon. I stood on the stage, looking out at the empty seats. Once, when I was in a hard-rock band—another life ago—I'd promised myself that one day I would perform on that stage. All summer I'd been visualizing it. Now it was happening.

Talking backstage before the audience showed up, we agreed that this was gravy. Even if we didn't win, we'd gotten further than we'd dreamed. We were going to enjoy the night. With that in mind, I put our set together without thinking about what the other teams were going to do. We didn't counter what other teams did, like some do in Slam. We went out showing what we felt was our best. Three group poems—two with all four of us in, one solo poem that spoke as much for its author—Cuffee—as it did for us and the rest of the Coyote Nation. We had more, but the set fell together naturally.

Other teams put on their game faces. Some played subtle mind games. We just took it all in and enjoyed ourselves.

Much has been said about the aftermath. Just like everything else, we didn't even know it was coming. While the storm built onstage with poets chastising the audience, we gathered in our traditional circle and just appreciated being together for the last time as a team—basking in the victory, sure, but basking more in the knowledge that we'd done the best performances of the summer that night.

When everything else had passed, I was taken back to the first day of Nationals, gathered on the stage in the Robinson Park with every Albuquerque poet there, showing the Slam family how we rolled and how deep we were. They didn't know that we had Sandia soil in our blood. They didn't know that the endless sky they saw leaving the airport was a part of us. Hakim and Cuffee hadn't been born in New Mexico, but they understood what it was to be Nuevo Mexicano.

In the end, we didn't win because we were the best. Team ABQ won because we were simply an extension of our community, and that community was over five hundred years in the making. On that Saturday night, in the Kiva, we called on ancestors to lift us on their shoulders, and they did. We honored them. We honored our community. And they honored us back. The Albuquerque Slam community came full circle from sending a team in 1995 to winning NPS 2005. Every ABQ Team contributed. The title wasn't won by five team members. It was won by a community of poets. Team ABQ '05 simply represented them. ■

Esmé Vaandrager
A m__i ng

We call it amazing:
— The lack of traffic
— The light pole against the sky
— The capacity for people to be so dumb.

In the presence of artwork,
We say amazing
Like the word could hold an o-mouthed choir
In its scarred, open palms.
Like it could hold bombs
In its mouth like marbles . . .
Bubbly "Wonderful, wonderful."

We call things a m__i ng
Until our enthusiasm is air in a fading balloon.
Thinner than skin.
A wet gel cap, half wrapper
For the object of approval,
— Encase it
— Make it somehow ours,

Thin
As the mark my lips make on your chin.

These are matters of faith
And opinion.
I just wonder about your
Amazing—
I am still waiting for the time when it catches
In your throat and I hear
Desperation,
The fear that someone will call our bluff

And laugh at our belief
In love

Perhaps I hold your hand too tight.
Perhaps you don't really listen.
Perhaps I am making a big deal out of nothing.

I just worry
When our footsteps echo hollow off museum walls
And you love
Every other painting
We pass. ▪

Kenn Rodriguez
Night of the Chihuahua

Heed my warnings, *gente*:
People, *El Noche del Chihuahua*,
The Night of the Chihuahua, approaches

The gory eve
when the wee dogs will come
to avenge the genocide of their forefathers

To counter the canine carnage
when their meat was harvested
& stuffed into tortillas

Long before one of their own
became a nationally recognized
spokesdog

Lobbying for the entrance
of the phrase *"Yo quiero Taco Bell"*
into the American lexicon

Taking its place alongside
the other Spanish words
which have been English-immersed

Macho, nachos, California, guacamole, salsa,
Colorado, Tabasco, Arizona, huevos rancheros
y con muchos gracias a Gerardo,

Rrrrrrrrrrrrr-Rico Suave!

Thus proving Proposition 227 was right,
proving that Spanish-speaking dogs
can survive the sink or swim mentality
& become productive members of Gringo society.

Yes, they can even make it . . . on television!

Ay, chihuahua!

Can no one see the clouds growing
on the horizon? The coming storm of their revenge,
when we will hear their battle cry,

"*VIVA GORDITAS!*" over and over again.

Soon, the cute little *perros*
and their Red-clad revolution
will have passed into TV oblivion.

Then and only then will *El Gran Jefe
de perros pequeños Mexicanos,*

El Ché-huahua,

pronounce his tribe's true intentions,
standing at a podium built from the ill-gained profits

of the PepsiCo Corporation,

monies culled from the pocket change of *gabachos*
who think the hot sauce they got at the drive-thru
is the worst of their future fears.

With blood red flags fluttering in the distance,
El Ché-huahua, will proclaim
the true nature of his televised *revolución,*

his voice growing into
an ominous baritone,
"*Yo . . . quiero . . .* HUMAN FLESH!"

AMERICAN FLESH!"

We will be no match for the little dogs
flowing over humanity wave after wave
to avenge their ancestors' passings,

to fulfill the prophecy
of the Great White Chihuahua,
a sign that they will soon be free,

and we, Chicanos, Gringos, Americanos alike,
will all fall, unable to run
because of our taco-induced weight,

unable to fight, because of our
hot sauce–induced flatulence,
unable to hide because
we have become the *gorditas*,

unable to stop the chihuahuas
from taking our place in the world.

Somewhere in the past
or maybe the future,
Charlton Heston's cries will be heard

with a slight Speedy Gonzales lilt,
screaming, as he is dragged off by members
of *El Ché-huahua's* Revolutionary Guard,

"*Gorditas*, they are made of people!
They are made of people!
THEY ARE MADE OF PEOPLE!" ■

Carlos Contreras

Common Ground

Written in conversation with Diane Thiel's "The Minefield."

1

We found ourselves,
some two generations   apart.
Not much in common,
still we'd played cat's cradle
with the same *trip   wires.*

2

She must have been young then.
Those stories ricocheting off her ears like enemy fire
off fellow fighters—
did it hurt?
I want to ask her . . .
Did you . . .
cry?
Knowing of the silence
wrapped like pine boxes in burdened banners,
but we were just pajama feet
POWs

Did it hurt?

3

Not when he hit but . . .
when he . . .
spoke?

I wouldn't be trying to
find out
more about her
as much as I would be
about myself;

like I said, we were generations
apart.
I haven't had time for my
heart to honorably discharge
my childhood memories.

4
Seems our fathers
shared common
ground—
defined themselves
with enemy lines
and never crossed too far
when recanting over dinner.

Mine
never snapped—
exploded on the inside
instead.
Like pigeons after an
Alka-Seltzer Breakfast,
his heart came home
but his mind never left it.

5
She may want to ask me,
did it hurt?
Not when he spoke,
but when he . . .
slept?
And we can compare stories
*"My dad would throw things,
noisy fm radios at kitchen walls."*
*"Mine would have slept through a fire in
the living room."*

Both fighting
fire with fire.
We'd know there was
no honorable discharge.
There is no way of assigning
demerits for angry
actions at this point because
Reality is
MIA
Defeat is begging on the
Corner
and somehow
They are still
Home.

6

Home,
a place where battlefields still exist,
and we've
taken off the pajamas
and adorned fatigues
because if there is
anything worth fighting for, it is them

7

She and I
may never know exactly
what happened—
where the mines within them
are hidden
and just what it takes
to explode. ▨

Hakim Bellamy
Wednesdays in Philly
Wednesday, April 13, 2005

City of Philadelphia Municipal Waste was what the truck read
I thought it funny on this awkwardly bright Wednesday that would have
    forced me to wear sunglasses anyway
That refuse to repass, ashes to ashes, dust . . .
To guts
Like what my father had
Sort of middle son of seven boys and a girl, and he spoke on behalf of the
    family
Gut to gut
Like grandmother whom eldest uncle speaks of as I stare outside grayed glass
    window in limo
You know . . .
"They were a great team. He worked from 4 a.m. 'til time to take her to work,
    finished the dinner she started, finished raising the children she
    started . . . relocated from sharecropping South to idealistic opportunity of
    the North . . . AND THEY FINISHED WHAT THEY STARTED!"
I went from gazing out grayed glass, to staring out stained glass, just so
I didn't have to see him laying there like that . . .
Guts?
Nah, I ain't got'em and what little bit I did have fell through the pit in
    the bottom of my stomach when Mom gave me the news
"They called for the family"

Fortunately I'm flying into Philly for some poetry
Unfortunately Father's father is fleeing this sphere
With no fear
'Cause "Ain't nobody loved Jesus like Grandpa loved Jesus . . ."
And it was time to meet him I suppose
Only two hours after I touched down that Wednesday
His body beaten by decades of doors of discrimination and doubt shut in his
    face
Pride built by kicking those same muthafuckin' doors off the hinges
Will, that sent seven of those kids of his to college and one to war
Past the extent of his elementary education

But "Ain't nobody treasured education like Grandpa treasured education"
And where there's a will, there's an obituary, and a eulogy, and tears, and
a way
Where there's a will and last testament
There's a way out of this element
But you gotta leave behind the weather-beaten, war torn carcass
Soul survivor
Friends and relatives as casualties
With a souvenir you left for an individual landfill
The body is garbage

Good thing it is Wednesday in Philadelphia
And like any GOOD celebration
The temple looks trashed afterwards
And the temple was a tornado of Tulips, Tigerlillies and Roses
Whirlwinds of harmonious vocals with just a dash of pain help to uplift the
church and everything in it except . . .
The guy at the eye of the storm
And in that stillness, that calm
I can see
Melodies from heaven raining down
Beading up as perspiration on the reverend's brow
As he ministers to the twister
"We come to celebrate this man's life, not mourn his death . . ."
And this is holy high heaven's last chance at a séance

Holy dances resemble rain dances
Cousins resemble uncles that they haven't seen in years
And won't
Until another death, birth or marriage

My father?
Resembles a son
When he breaks down, giving in to emotion for the first time in my twenty-six-year-
old eyes
And Grandpa
He resembles the nobility of my gene pool
Work ethic and integrity

His body symbolic of success
The American Dream before the perversion that left the foul taste of soiled
    sheets in the mouths of the American Public
But the only thing Grandpa tastes now is victory
The choir erupts into "When the Saints Go Marching In . . ."
And that embalmed grin
On his face, just seems to get a little wider
Off to a better party than the temple he left
His earthly temple
Probably more trashed by the cancer than the dancing
See
Grandpa didn't go out much
He preferred family gatherings and weekday worship services
Good eats and good peeps
Who all share good words about him now . . .
But this
Is one of those rare cases when they actually had good things to say about
    the person BEFORE they died too . . .
And there it is . . .
I finally had the guts to say it.

He died . . .
After not only giving me life, but a lifestyle
With style
From his caps and top hats to Cadillacs
He died . . .
Leaving me to write rhymes and scribe eyes for the blind
He died . . .
To show me that my light can still shine . . .
After I die
So I write
The body of work that they can't dispose of, erase or take at my wake . . .
I create
Faith, beauty, thought, love, a legacy

Like
Wednesdays in Philly, just me and Grandpop. ■

Chantal Foster

Albuquerque and NPS 2005

Slam poetry fan and ardent Albuquerque booster, Chantal Foster is also founder of www.dukecityfix.com.

> *"Last night, hundreds of Slam poets descended on Albuquerque like beautiful swarms of multicultural bliss. Slammers from the Carolinas, slammers from Chicago, even a slam group from France, wow, France. Hundreds of street-scene poets making rhymes so powerful, it'll make your bones go hollow.*
>
> *Albuquerque, the poet warriors are here."*

That's what I wrote in August 2005 at the start of the National Poetry Slam Finals held in Albuquerque. Dusty, underdog Albuquerque opening our arms to a group of people who opened theirs right back—the Slam poets. Slam poets who showered our city with underground love so strong we had to wear turtlenecks to cover up the hickeys . . .

It was a week that filled the streets of Albuquerque with grit and magic and fire. Erotic poetry, feminist poetry, nerd poetry, and more. I heard tales of midnight skinny-dipping poets and crosstown rivalries playing out like electricity on a Route 66 stage. The entire Duke City felt it. And for once, we felt good about our role in making it happen—HERE.

IN OUR CITY.

Sure, our edges are scrappy. Admittedly, we've got some work to do. But in Albuquerque, what you see is what you get, and we'll tell you this straight up and then hand you a beer and a tamale. So come sit around the bonfire, Albuquerque, and toast to the future. A future we saw in the faces of our fire-wielding, poet-warrior guests.

The era of "The City Real" is coming. And it's so palpable you could gnaw on it like a tasty pork rib and for the first time in a long time, feel full. ▪

Henry Sampson

Some Recollections of the National Poetry Slam, Albuquerque, 2005

Vice-president of Poetry Slam, Inc. (PSi), Henry Sampson was the tournament director for NPS 2005.

I headed to Albuquerque on a United flight out of O'Hare International Airport at 10:00 a.m. on Monday, August 8, 2005, for the National Poetry Slam, an exciting event for me. I have attended poetry slams in Chicago since early 1990 and experienced my first national event in 1991, when Marc Smith brought eight teams to Chicago for the second of these annual tournaments. By the time the next nationals came to Chicago in 1997, I had helped to organize a regional slam event and was one of the principal hosts for the 1999 National Poetry Slam. That involvement began my work with the Executive Council of Poetry Slam, Inc., a relatively young organization, incorporated in 1997.

Chicago NPS 1997 helped shape a future direction for PSi. Previously, when a city hosted nationals, the organizers were fairly free to propose changes in rules, the number of teams, or the set up of the bouts. That resulted in some very uneven results from year to year, as some cities like Asheville and Ann Arbor did a tremendous amount of preparation and worked from a highly refined set of organizational skills to execute excellent plans. Other cities did not show the same level of skill.

The Executive Council of Poetry Slam, Inc. instituted changes over the space of a couple of years that divided the responsibilities for each national event between the host city and PSi. This is how I found myself more than a little involved with the organizers of the Albuquerque NPS. I have served as the tournament director since 2002, and as the vice-president of Poetry Slam, Inc. I helped negotiate the contract with the host city.

My flight arrived on time, and in the cab, I asked the driver for a good spot for breakfast. His immediate response was Garcia's Kitchen (Danny Solis recommended the Barelas Coffeehouse!). We were off to a good start. The cabdriver asked what brought me to Albuquerque, and I told him we were there for the National Poetry Slam. He had heard about it! An even better start.

The 2004 National Poetry Slam had been a disappointment in many ways, the most obvious being the dismal size of the audiences throughout the week, a direct result of poor marketing on the part of the host city. For Albuquerque, Don McIver submitted Albuquerque's Marketing Plan to the Executive Council with a timeline that ran from April 2003 up to the planned articles due to appear in August 2005—a thorough document that was obviously very well executed.

Albuquerque demonstrated, probably better than any NPS before it, and probably any since then, the right combination of leadership, charisma, and skills to run a national literary event. My take is that this success started with Danny Solis. Danny has always been an impressive member of the spoken-word community, winning several national titles, and providing a strong voice within the community. As the artistic director for the Albuquerque event, Danny has the experience and the artistic vision, and he brought on board an excellent team: Don McIver, SlamMaster, host of poetry events in Albuquerque, and a very capable marketing guy; Susan McAllister, the budget, finance, and fundraising guru; and Maresa Thompson, who seemed to keep everything well-organized. Albuquerque's efforts were successful enough that the organizers did not need to use an available $10,000 pre-event loan from Poetry Slam, Inc. to cover their early expenses—a positive and healthy sign.

One of the most impressive aspects of the 2005 National Poetry Slam was the host city's alliance with the National Hispanic Cultural Center (NHCC). Several people on the Executive Council of Poetry Slam, Inc. took a tour of the facilities before the kickoff ceremonies. I was impressed not only with the wonderful facilities and the several different size theaters available for the Albuquerque crew to use, but also by the accessibility and friendliness of the entire staff of the NHCC. NHCC hosted an official news conference with the mayor, an opening event for poets the night before the tournament began, and numerous events at several venues throughout the week, including stepping up to host an unscheduled semifinal bout when the need arose.

Oftentimes the national organizers are understandably burned out and need time to gather their wits, but the Albuquerque crew has stayed involved and is now impacting the larger national poetry scene. Don has run for, and won, a seat on the Executive Council of Poetry Slam, Inc. and has recently taken a position as the chair of the Membership Committee. Susan helped the Austin National Poetry Slam organizers in 2007 as a finance coordinator and is helping raise funds for the first ever Women's Poetry Slam in March 2008.

The most difficult part of being in Albuquerque was deciding whether to have breakfast at Garcia's or the Barelas Coffeehouse each day! ◼

Susan McAllister

Thank You/Acknowledgments

This book, beginning to end, celebrates community and the time, talent, and energy it took to build it. It is important to recognize, though, that individual communities grow within a larger framework, engaging with organizations outside their sphere, influenced by and influencing their city, their state, the country . . . Everyone involved with NPS 2005 recognizes that we are fortunate to have the benefit of an engaged and supportive "larger community."

The following may look like a laundry list, but in one way or another, every one of these businesses, individuals, foundations, civic organizations, and politicians supported the growing Slam community and contributed to making NPS 2005 successful. In many, many cases the support continues. Thank them whenever you can. Really.

These are the real community builders in New Mexico:

The New Mexico State Legislature, Governor Bill
  Richardson, and Representative Mimi Stewart
City of Albuquerque and Mayor Martin Chávez
Bernalillo County
Harwood Art Center and Escuela del Sol Montessori
Albuquerque Convention and Visitors Bureau
National Hispanic Cultural Center
Urban Enhancement Trust Fund
McCune Charitable Foundation
New Mexico Arts
A Room of Her Own Foundation
Don Mickey Designs
KUNM

Cathey Miller

Hotel Blue

La Posada

Albuquerque the Magazine

Puccini's Golden West Saloon

Launchpad

Flying Star

El Rey Theater

OPM Nightclub

National Institute of Flamenco

Albuquerque City Councilor Eric Griego

AbqARTS

Alibi

Seventh Goddess

New Mexico Voice

Crosswinds Weekly

Adventures in Advertising and Michael Madanick

Albuquerque Poetry Slam Council

Untitled Fine Arts Services

Vortex Theatre

Blue Dragon Coffeehouse

Natural Sound

Bookworks

Tricklock Company

Outpost Performance Space

New Mexico CultureNet

Southwest Airlines

Hyatt Regency Tamaya Resort and Spa

Graze by Jennifer James

Rainbow Ryders Hot Air Balloon Company

Downtown Action Team

Martha's Body Bueno

Pueblo Loft

Two Wheel Drive, Inc.

Hinkle Family Fun Center

One Connect IP

Angel Alley

Off Center Community Arts

New Mexico Sports and Wellness

Day Spa at Serenity Gardens

Winning Coffee Co.

Adobe Silver at Naranjo Gallery of Art

Out ch'Yonda

Herbs Etc.

Marble Street Studio

Ben E. Keith Co.

Calpulli Ehecatl Aztec Dancers

Lumpkin Family Foundation

Deborah Reese

All our fabulous volunteers ▪

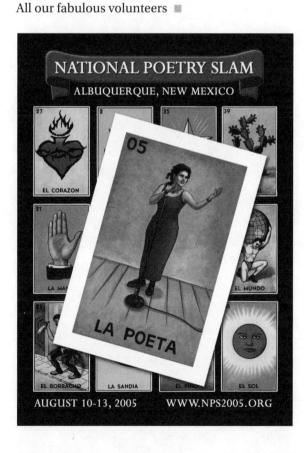

Figure 22. NPS 2005 Postcard. *Courtesy of Cathey Miller, artist, and Maresa Thompson, graphic designer*

Chapter Six

ABQ Aftermath

Susan McAllister

Aftermath: The Arts Community

Early on Sunday afternoon, as NPS 2005 was winding down, the organizers drifted into the hotel headquarters room without anyone having suggested we meet. For the first time in months, there was nothing NPS related that we had to do, but we were still in a state of hyper-organizing and meeting was our habit. We talked a little about the antics onstage the night before, about the incredible success of our hometown team, about what parts of our lives, long neglected, we had to get back to, and about being glad it was over but sad at the same time. We didn't talk about things we had to finish up; that afternoon no one was in any hurry.

As Sunday wore on visiting poets made their way to the airport, we gathered all the stuff of organizing that was strewn around, and we left the hotel assuming the adventure was over. But during the next few weeks each of us realized something: Albuquerque was different. It was intangibly shifted, and somehow changed.

Four of the NPS organizers formed the International Poetry Institute (IPI), realizing that the shift, that change, was part of why we worked so long and hard on Nationals. It was what we wanted to hold on to, support, run with. We called it "the bounce," and it strengthened our core belief that poetry is a force, and people are hungry for it.

IPI embraces four interrelated programming branches: production, education, publishing, and community support.

In the year and a half since Nationals we have been working in each area. IPI was cosponsor of writing workshops at Sequoia in Spring 2006, the Threatened Languages Poetry Reading at Harwood in January 2007, and the Mid School Slam at NHCC in April 2007. We are working with Harwood and the University of New Mexico to revitalize the Albuquerque Poetry Festival. In the midst of all that, we have created this book as a way of recording where we came from, and where we're going. ■

Becky Holtzman

Artists and NPS

Organizer, volunteer, and audience member at NPS 2005, Becky Holtzman created the Sacred Heart linocut based on the NPS 2005 logo.

As a visual artist, I've often turned to poetry—all kinds—to inform and push my own work. In considering Slam, what it is, how it functions, I think it might be the kinetic sculpture of poetry. Slam takes up space, and it doesn't usually close into the pages of a book. It's more than a poem read aloud; it's poetry as a living thing, fed on a poet's finesse, and on audience receptivity. Because in Slam, part of the art is the poet taking the breath of her audience in, shaping it into words, and exhaling it back out to that audience: transformed. ▩

Figure 23. Sacred Heart Linocut Inspired by NPS 2005 Logo. *Courtesy of Becky Holtzman*

Don McIver

Aftermath: The Poetry Community

Sometimes I have to remember that everything is not all peachy, not always golden, not always everybody getting along, liking each other. Sometimes I remember that communities, like families, fight, squabble, and dislike each other, and that is how I know, at times, that ABQ has a strong poetry community.

I was standing in line at a play in January in the northeast heights, and this man came up to me. I didn't know him, yet I smiled.

"You're Don McIver, right?"

"Yeah, I am."

"You know I just got to say, congratulations. You guys did an amazing job with Nationals. Are you planning on doing it again?"

It was not the first time I'd heard the question since the gear was broken down, the lights turned off at the Kiva Auditorium. Every time I bike by Hotel Blue, I look up at the marquee and remember it saying, "Welcome to the National Poetry Slam." NPS 2005 was an event that changed my life, changed Albuquerque's life.

Overall, hosting the Nationals was a positive experience not only for the poets and organizers involved but the city overall. Prior to hosting Nationals, there was one entity, called ABQ Slams. ABQ Slam's job was to ensure that the local slams were fair and well-attended. Prior to Nationals, a few of us stepped away from ABQ Slams to work for NPS 2005. Once Nationals was over, we stepped back in.

In August we added another slam to our three per month schedule and now have a slam a week, all coordinated and run by ABQ Slams. In October, we moved our bar reading to a new venue because they gave us a better deal, and the attendance has steadily increased. Prior to Nationals, I speculated that attendance at slams would go down because we were adding another slam and didn't have the draw of Nationals anymore. I'm glad to report I was wrong. All four slams draw well, with full sign-up lists and good crowds. To date, we've had eighty-five different poets who've slammed this year. Admittedly forty of those poets (for a variety of reasons) have only slammed once all year, but that means there are forty-five different poets who slam on a regular basis.

Some of the outreach we did prior to Nationals has continued. A few of the team and community members were working with schools prior to Nationals and continue doing that important work. Other team members began working in different schools as well. In April 2006, we sent the first citywide youth team to Brave New Voices in New York City.

There are now four area high schools and a few middle schools that are being introduced to Slam. In April 2007, we hosted the second Middle School Poetry Slam. In addition, we've done more outreach at the college level, including visiting classes regularly and hosting a College Union Slam on a regular basis and sending teams to the national competition. The University of New Mexico now offers a "Spoken Word" class in the English Department. Created with our input and feedback, we hope to create a "Spoken Word" thread as part of UNM's curriculum.

In two 2005 year-end summaries (one in December and one in January), the *Alibi* honored NPS 2005 as one of the bright spots of the year and one of the top ten arts events. Our local arts organization, the Albuquerque Arts Alliance, awarded us the Bravos Award for best theatre arts event of the past year. On a personal level, I was named as one of the "40 Under 40" by the *New Mexico Business Weekly* and got to see my first book come out in November, both largely due to my work on Nationals.

We've had our ups and downs personally throughout the year, but Slam continues. The NPS 2005 crew has largely disbanded, but some have moved on to the International Poetry Institute, an organization that hopes to provide a venue for page and stage poets: the *Poet's Plaza Magazine* and an all-inclusive poetry library. There's been talk about hosting the Individual World Poetry Slam (IWPS), College Unions, Brave New Voices, the Women of the World (WOW) Poetry Slam, or even another NPS, but nothing's definitive.

The year 2005 will be memorable for many of us in Albuquerque. As the Slam season winds down each year, we look forward to picking a new team and burdening them with the task of retrieving the trophy. Because of Nationals, every year's team carries the hopes and dreams of an entire city, not an easy burden to live with, but not a bad one either. ▪

Arts Alliance

2006 Bravos Award in Theatre Arts

Albuquerque's arts advocacy organization, Arts Alliance hosts a yearly award for the best of the arts.

An annual awards celebration that honors excellence in the Albuquerque arts community, the Arts Alliance Bravos Awards began in 1985 with thirty artists and friends in attendance. The annual awards dinner now attracts hundreds of guests, and the recipients are honored throughout the year. Bravos celebrates the best in all of the arts disciplines: visual, dance, music, theater, and literary.

The 2005 National Poetry Slam, the largest performance poetry festival in the world, was held in Albuquerque. The event captivated capacity crowds with its mixture of performance, competition, and audience participation. For four days in August, Albuquerque played host to teams of Slam poets (and their supporters) from around the country and the world, culminating in the local team winning the event before an audience of more than 2,300. The Slam committee—Danny Solis (chair/artistic director), Don McIver (publicity director/Webmaster), Susan McAllister (chief financial officer), and Maresa Thompson (meeting planner/graphic designer)—began planning the event in the fall of 2002. Their efforts certainly paid off, bringing recognition to the Duke City as a city appreciative and welcoming of poetry and the creative people who make it. ■

Don McIver
Word-Sure Boy

Word-sure boy sure of words is gone now.
He's gone, grown-up, replaced.
Cell by cell by cell by cell he's been replaced twofold times,
All that's left are memories.

Though you had no way of knowing,
This was the first time he ever felt like he belonged;
He found his place,
So he made sure every one else stayed in theirs.

Word-sure boy sure of words.
Say things no one else will say,
Harass, berate, belittle, mock
Anyone who won't conform to his notion
Of being the big cheese in the Burger King kitchen;
The go-to guy for odd jobs, getting even.
How could he—word-sure boy—bully with his size?
Rail thin and awkwardly uncomfortable.
Barely six feet tall and one fifty.

Word-sure boy—sure of words
should've been more sensitive to differences,
How much like the rest of them you were.
He should've known better.
Instead, he joked,
Asking how things are going for you—African-American-Black,
And your lily-white-anglo wife.
He joked,
"How do you stop five black guys from raping a white woman?"
Never mind the obvious offense.
That was not the point,
Though it was.

Though you had no game,
He told the joke anyway

To let you know he didn't see you as Black, Colored.
How many other jokes did other people tell?
You, the only Colored, Negro employee
At a Burger King in the suburbs?
Total population of minorities, not ten percent.

Word-sure boy sure of words, isn't from the streets,
Clichéd explanations of why some people are racist and others aren't.
From the south, an easy—too easy—stereotype of racist learning.
He had a dog named Sambo
And his blue-blood grandmother had a live-in maid named Lizzy Tee for forty years.

Yet word-sure boy was also from the rural south,
Colored lines blurring,
And Curtis and Johnny called him their "best friend."
Word-sure boy dated outside his race,
But he never called her "nigger."

Maybe it wasn't about the color of your skin?
Maybe it was more about your gender, your personality, your competence
And he used your skin color to keep you down:
To let you know your place?

I don't know.
I don't even know, anymore.
That boy, that punk, that mouthy, arrogant,
Unapologetic word-sure boy
Who inhabited this body,
Whose cells have been replaced, twofold times.
But memories.
They won't go away.
Memories never go
Away.
These are the cells that aren't replaced.
They remember.

Kenn Rodriguez

Where Do We Go from Here—after the 2005 Championship

The Slam season after the 2005 championship was probably the most competitive since the early days of Slam in Albuquerque. There were plenty of people who came out of the woodwork to make things interesting. You had National Poetry Slam volunteers, young and old, you had audience members, and you had slammers who'd been trying for years to make it into finals. The 2006 team strived to have its own identity. And it did.

The '06 team was dubbed *"la familia"* by Esmé Vaandrager, who was a full member this time around. Watching her and Jessica Lopez, Lee Francis, Damien Flores, and our other '05 returnee Hakim Bellamy was both a privilege and a pleasure. My seat wasn't too far away either—I was again selected as coach (along with Esmé, who was eventually voted onto the team). Preparing with them was as much fun as working with the '05 team.

Watching these five work and play, you saw a *familia*. A lot of time notions like this are bypassed by the first road trip, but Team ABQ '06 never frayed at the edges. Team '06 was emblematic of the ABQ scene, post-'05.

Hakim and Damien could be considered the veterans of the team. Damien had already been slamming for five years. Hakim was only in his second full year of slamming and had dominated, giving him vet status. Esmé, like Damien, was young but already an old hand at Slam. Even Jessica and Lee were newcomers only in the amount of time they'd spent in Slam. For a lot of us, 2006 began a transition. The old-timers—Don McIver, Danny Solis, myself—are welcoming in newcomers and new blood. We've even got organizational vets like Susan McAllister, Maresa Thompson, and Mikaela Renz from the 2005 organizing committee coming out to help run things now.

One of the themes from 2005 was that Team ABQ was not just the people on the team, but the entire community. Now that's a utopian statement, and while it may not have been 100 percent what ABQ was about, it's always been what we've strived for.

In 2006 and going forward, it seems like ABQ Slam is headed in a new, yet familiar direction. The 2007 slam-off had more new slammers involved than ever before. As of this writing, eight slammers have been chosen for the finals stage, and more than half have never performed on a finals stage. I don't have any more insight to the future than any other ABQ poet, but I can tell you this: I'm not worried. The foundation is set. The house can now safely be built. ▪

Kenn Rodriguez
Rock 'n' Roll
A reading from the gospel of rock 'n' roll, book 13, chapter 25Or6t04, verse 666.

"Rock 'n' roll is dead," the DJ said.
They placed a microchip in his head,
forced him to play Creed and Simply Red,
bleeding from the speakers like satanic messages from Barney.

Well, hell . . . I'd heard Barney is the Messiah,
Barney is gay, Barney is Elvis, Barney is just
Mick Jagger in disguise.
Imagine Barney singing "Jumping Jack Flash, he's a gas, gas, gas."

Imagine Kurt Cobain and Marvin Gaye coming back
covering "Ebony and Ivory" without any irony.
I'll bet MTV could turn them into
supergodrockstars if they wanted to.

Yeah, people would love them, buy their albums,
go to their reunion shows, watch their videos.
People would love them like they were the

StoneTempleAudioDestiny'sPilotsoftheSlaveStoneAgeNelly.
MTV would resurrect them! They'd play Woodstock 2010!
People would flock to them
like sheep led to the slaughter for rock 'n' roll, for
rock 'n' roll?

How tiresome. I'm disgusted.
I'm embarrassed to say that as a teenager
I raised my hand with the index finger & pinky
pointed straight into the air when
I could've been listening to something
cool.

I coulda been a punk rocker, singin'
"Twen'y twen'y twen'y fo'r hours to go/I Wanna Be Sedated . . ."

coulda painted my nails black, worn eyeliner to school &
been challenged to fights by the jocks every day at lunchtime

coulda sprayed my hair up into a tumbleweed,
worn ripped fatigues & old combat boots
listened to The Cure, The Smiths, Siouxsie, Bauhaus!
Yeah! Hey DJ! Play "Bela Lugosi is Dead!"

No . . . Rock 'n' roll is dead.

We barely noticed.
Led Zeppelin, Lynrd Skynrd, Mötley Crüe—they're all dead. Now
Alice Cooper plays golf, Ozzy's on reality TV,
& Axl Rose is sticking crystals up his bum in Sedona or Santa Fe.

Hey that's all the radio would play back in 1988.
Now it's too late for them or you or me.

Everybody knows rock 'n' roll is dead.

Everybody knows rock 'n' roll died the minute
David Lee Roth left Van Halen.
Everybody knows rock 'n' roll died the minute
Joey Ramone left this planet.
Everybody knows rock 'n' roll died the minute
Ricky Martin swiveled his hips &
sang the words
"Livin'
La Vida
Loca."

Rock 'n' roll is dead, folks, & nothing can save us.

Putting David Lee Roth up on the cross will not save us.
Putting Sammy Hagar up on the cross will not redeem us.

Putting that . . . third singer guy . . . from Van Halen?
you know . . .

What's his Name!

Putting his skinny ass up on the cross will not forgive our sins.

Yes, rock 'n' roll is dead, folks! Rock 'n' roll is dead!
But Joey Ramone

Joey Ramone
lives
on. ■

Note: This poem was reworked from an original version. I won my very first poetry slam at the Fabulous Dingo Bar with the original version of the poem. I also caught the ear of Bob Holman, who gave me some praise for it. It was because of that poem that I continued as a Slam poet. This new version helped me get on the 2005 ABQ Poetry Slam Team. So in a way it helped me close my own poetry circle.

Jessica Lopez
Billie's Blues Are Mine
*Member of the 2006 and 2007 Albuquerque Slam teams, Jessica Lopez
was a founding member of New Mexico Poetry Tangents and coeditor of*
Earthships: A New Mecca Poetry Anthology.

My gardenia scented getaway
Suicide not for fame
Dulling color fades today
I'm no Sylvia Plath mama
Sexy Anne Sexton
Tragic Ophelia
Won't go out mad martyr style
But sometimes the slide
Of silky fingers collide with my sensibilities
Sing a song of the lovely siren
That is the Lady
The smoky sad jazz of Billie beckons me
Blue, deep, onyx sea palette
Watery grave
My gardenia scented getaway

The greasy trombone and melodic
Boom of bass guitar
Light fingers play piano keys
Tap in Morse code the misery
Through music
Honey butter songstress
The bleeding heart of Billie's mantra
My gardenia scented homegirl

Sheets cover the windows
Keep the room cool and dark
When La Catrina speaks, bleached bone and bourgeois
Her skeletal thin-skinned hand soothes me

She hums death dreams
Lulls me to sleep
Smooth jazz reprieve
Silky fingers of subjugation offer rest from the rage
That burns the heart
Chatters away my brain
Thumps my sleep out from its groove
The xylophone of my rib cage
Cradle to the downcast heart
Silly moon

So many odes to that old girl have they made!
Miss Holiday
A good morning to heartache
In her solitude going bad
Singing away like no one can
My sickness of sadness

You Frida lady
Lady Lazarus
Supernova woman
Posturing pain
Whispering
Muerto, muerto, muerto
Llorona leave me be
Prayers allow me to channel
The power of the *Chola Loca*
High hair devil-may-care
Barrio bitch
Something is passing through these veins again
Haunting my heart
Hopelessly hypnotic
A Homeric epic needing release
Heroin overdose all dressed up and nowhere to go
Needling straight to the cardiac arrest

Slipping the noose around the songbird's neck
Snap shut the nightingale
Who will sing less and less and less

Knowing this day will come again
And I will do as Dylan says and
Rage, rage against the dying of the light
And only if
How I wish
Wonder if
His villanelle encompasses the ladies too
And not just the fathers and deaths of old men

Tomorrow will be a Zack de la Rocha day
Charles Bukowski, Diane Wakoski
A *pinche puta* Cisneros day
Tomorrow will be walk on Washington
Bulldowg battle along the border
A fight for the brown
But today
I sit in the lovely gray
The cleansing rain
That is Lady Day ■

Lee Francis

Polonius's Advice to His Son (the Remix)

Member of the 2006 Albuquerque Slam Team, Lee Francis was cohost of
Blue Dragon II Poetry Slam.

Yet here Laertes! Aboard, aboard for shame!
The wind sits in the shoulder of your sail
And you are stayed for. There: my blessing with thee—
—Polonius, Hamlet, *Act 1, Scene 3*

If I were Polonius giving words to my son
    I would tell him of the world
    and all the beauty therein
    I would tell him of the stones and the trees
    and point to them and say to him that
    "Those are your beginnings, my child;
    remember everything is connected"
    I would tell him of the sky and the stars
    and point to them and say to him that
    "Those are your limits, my child,
    and anyone who tries to tell you otherwise
    should be cast from your side"
If I were Polonius giving words to my son
    I would tell him to make friends easily
    to laugh and play like he was a child
    without fear of falling
    I would tell him to gather his friends close
    and to give his heart freely to all
    but that only the number he can count
    on one hand will be willing to give their
    hearts in return
If I were Polonius giving words to my son
    I would tell him to live in peace
    to calm his soul with words and thoughts
    and looks at another's shoes so he
    understands their travels

        but
        that there are times when righteousness
        is called for and when the trumpet sounds
        that he will not shy away from the blade
        but wield it skillfully to defend those
        who have no other to fight for them
If I were Polonius giving words to my son
        I would tell him to eat well
        and never turn down a meal
        to try everything even if it still moving
        because although he may grow fat
        the stories are well worth it
        I would tell him to spend his money
        freely and extravagantly on everyone he knows
        to never keep tabs and not to worry
        about bad credit because the credit agency
        is gonna fuck you no matter what
        If I were Polonius giving words to my son
        I would tell him that there are
        many terrible days out there
        that many times he will cry at night
        because of the
        intolerable cruelties that human beings
        can visit upon one another
        but each day brings a new promise
        and that this too shall pass away
        And when things get real bad

        and they will

        I will tell him to rent two movies
        One—*The Grapes of Wrath* and
        Two—*Mary Poppins*
        The first because twenty minutes in
        he will know that things may be bad

but at least he is better off than

a homeless farmer during the depression

and the second because

nothing cheers you up faster

than singing dancing chimney sweeps

If I were Polonius giving words to my son

    I would tell him the hardest lesson I know

    is that everything is temporary

    even me

And if I were Polonius giving words to my son

    I would tell him of the world

    and the amazing adventures he will have

    I would tell him to remember to floss, to remember to be grateful, to use a turn
signal, to say thank you, to share, to eat his broccoli, to say his prayers, to think
good thoughts, to remember the good and forget the bad, to enjoy each moment
as if it were his last, and I would tell him this above all:

    To thine own self be true

    and it must follow, my beautiful boy, as the night the day

    Thou canst not then be false to any man.

    Farewell, my wonderful, amazing child, my blessing season this in thee. ▪

Damien Flores

UNM Spoken Word and College Unions Poetry Slam Invitational (CUPSI)

Albuquerque poet and member of the 2005 and 2007 UNM Slam teams from the University of New Mexico, Damien Flores was a member of the 2006 Albuquerque Slam Team and is organizing the College Union Poetry Slam Invitational in Albuquerque in 2008.

In the fall of 2003, Poetry Slam inevitably made its appearance at the University of New Mexico (UNM). Angela Williams, a veteran of the Albuquerque Poetry Slam Team, had spearheaded a poetry slam club while a student at Albuquerque High School, and she took the same initiative at the university. With the help of another spoken word aficionado, Sari Krosinsky, Williams created a chartered organization under the name Word Revolution, which put together various free events at UNM. Open mics and poetry slams were not uncommon in the Student Union Building as Word Revolution claimed its home at the coffee counter, Higher Grounds, and took on a new personality with a shorter, catchier name, Word Rev.

The following semester, Word Rev selected a poetry slam team to represent the University of New Mexico at the College Unions Poetry Slam Invitational (CUPSI), the collegiate equivalent of the National Poetry Slam, held at the University of California at Berkeley that year. To determine who was on the team, Word Rev held a self-dubbed "Slam-Off," open to all students, staff, and faculty of both UNM and TVI (now Central New Mexico Community College). When the night ended, the first UNM Slam Team had been formed and was comprised of five undergraduate students, the Word

Rev champion Carlos Contreras, Aaron Cuffee, Libby Kelly, and Mark Fischer, with Angela Williams as the alternate and Kenn Rodriguez as coach.

From 2004 at UC-Berkeley to 2005 in Westchester, Pennsylvania, UNM's talent and reputation grew. In 2006, Word Rev, made up of Hakim Bellamy, Carlos Contreras, Aaron Cuffee, and me, drove to San Marcos for CUPSI, hosted by Texas State University. There in Texas, we dominated our preliminary bouts with individual poems and got a perfect score for a collaborative poem all four members performed together to get to finals. We performed all collaborative poems as a team in finals and wound up taking first place—a second National Championship for Albuquerque and a first for the University of New Mexico.

The 2007 CUPSI was at Eastern Michigan University and UNM Word Rev is under a new name: Loboslam. With the same organizing crew from the previous year and a new academic advisor, Levi Romero, Loboslam defended its title in April, and continues to provide UNM students with free events, readings, and poetry slams. Several Loboslam members are volunteer teachers and writing instructors around the local community, specializing in youth-oriented writing and performance workshops as an outlet for young frustration. Loboslam has also won the bid to host the 2008 CUPSI at the University of New Mexico.

Loboslam was born in the spirit of the word and raised in the arms of 'Burque. It will continue to grow like a cottonwood in the center of campus, with mud as ancient ink and notebook pages as its whispering leaves, falling for those who care to sit beneath its shade and read and listen. ■

Damien Flores
Una Novena pa la Tierra

There was dirt in their blood at birth.
They slid from their mothers' wombs
across the face of the Rio Grande
where there is no deep kiss
of minnows and mud
in a river that once
pulsed the bosque
and held cities
captive like stained water
in her hands.

The Rio Grande
flooded every year,
drowning up to downtown
just high enough to ruin
the politicos' suits.

They didn't notice the dirt
was coming back to them.
That the river was a messenger,
a *novena* of mud.

The land reclaiming its men.

A mother returned for her sons
after years dead.

And they dammed off the river,
blocked and diverted her fury
for its supplication of this holy dirt.

La tierra santisima.

Blocked her like a menstrual flow.

Men need to control their women
how they can,
so they were taught by their fathers.
They ripped the moon from
her waters,
shattered it with fallen limbs
when night was not watching
and buried its pieces
within the bosque.

Forced among the roots
of salt cedars and Chinese elms
gorging on the soil.
While the cottonwoods
swallowed moonlight
and shined it back from
gnarled branches,
shaky as the grip of a *viejita*,
gave the light back to
her shores and to the dirt.

They could not ignore their blood clotting,
broken stones

culled from the mountains
that were once their ancestors

who were once the lands
they now owned,
and governed

who were the names
they'd grown ashamed of.

That dirt which became
their district lines,
their voter precincts

Mud twisted into
that bastard tongue
with which they speak to money.
That bastard tongue
with which they whisper prayers
to their god
who was never theirs.
And they burned the bosque,
cast lightning
from city hall
into the river.

They had never seen
the face of the water burn
so miraculously.

Levi Romero

The UNM Spoken Word Initiative

A northern New Mexico poet, Levi Romero is also a creative writing professor at the University of New Mexico.

In the fall of 2003 University of New Mexico (UNM) students and local Albuquerque Slam poets Angela Williams and Sara Krosinky created a school-chartered organization under the name Word Revolution (Word Rev) to host open mics and slams on campus. The following semester, Word Rev selected a slam team comprised of five students to represent UNM at the College Unions Poetry Slam Invitational at the University of California at Berkeley. Since its inception, Word Rev has had two other leaders, Libby Kelly and current student and Albuquerque Slam poet Damien Flores.

In the fall '06 semester the English Department began a Spoken Word Initiative spearheaded by instructor Kevin Cassell and UNM Slam Team members Hakim Bellamy, Carlos Contreras, Aaron Cuffee, and Damien Flores. The effort produced The Spoken Word, a genre studies class that I teach as a creative writing instructor. The Spoken Word Initiative aims to be inclusive of the Albuquerque and New Mexico spoken word community within the university environment. Loboslam (previously Word Rev) continues to participate in local and national competitions. Loboslam members are also volunteer teachers and writing instructors around the local community specializing in youth-oriented writing and performance workshops. ▪

Levi Romero
New and Rejected Works

I watched a dropped
metallic lavender colored '66 LeMans
pulling out of the AutoZone onto Sunset
sporting 5/60's, Cragars, curb feelers, and rabbit ears

rabbit ears?

simón, a true period piece, *ese!*

a mid-seventies testament
a real gem of the Sunday afternoon cruise
an Ichi Coo Park, everyone's-eyes-on-it
carwash bitchin'
piece-of-ass scoring *ranfla*

what does all this all mean?

what true literary aficionado
could understand or bare even the slightest interest
in this ghost-patterned paint, chrome and rubber observation?

will this poem
be allowed to exist
alongside other genres of poetry?

to say the least of its highly improbable publication possibilities
in reputable, established "American" literary journals
that hold, in their editorial exercising power
the ability to affirm and measure
a writer's worthwhile poetic existence

no, probably not

yet, that bumper scraping cruiser
dressed in accessories from a past era

and cruising down the street literally naked
to the general public mind
was nothing but *pura poesia* to me

a statement of personal taste
much as other's interest akin to stamp collecting,
gun and knife shows or extravagant doll exhibits

as well as, say, literary journal subscriptions
for those who must have their poetic fix
mailed to them every month,
curbing an appetite for the compositional qualities
and technical structuring of a language
that works best with a certain degree of abstraction

is this poem abstract enough?

does it carry a central theme engaging a universal dialogue?
is it Eastern enough to satisfy the taste of the self-absorbent
intellectually sophisticated Western palette?

will the U.S. poet laureate nod his head in approval
and suggest that it at least be considered
placed next to the greatest poems ever written
about cats curled up on a windowsill?

hmmm, maybe it's a little bit too literal
too barrio, too East LA-ish
or just too Aztlanish

there are, of course, some great literary enthusiasts
that could easily decipher the blue-dot
'67 Cougar taillight blinking like a Christmas tree *carucha*,
with the boogie-woogie *rolas* riffing
out've a set of organ pipes,
and a dashboard saint protecting us
from that which does not understand us,
chain steering wheeled chariot

with the red lights flashing in the mirror

   red lights flashing in the mirror?
    maybe it's the poetry police!
     ¡ponte truchas, carnal!

great literary enthusiasts who can't even read
who do not have subscriptions to anything of self-interest
because nothing they were ever given to read
made sense to them either

great literary enthusiasts holed up in a lockup facility
who sit waiting for their final sentence to be read to them
who without explanation or implication are told
we are simply following due process

whose hearts and souls and spirits and lives
have been censored by mainstream off-the-shelf everything
and who were given instead the concrete void of insulin
Metrazol electricity
hydrotherapy, psychotherapy
ping-pong & amnesia

oops, now, how did that get in there?

how come nothing in the great american poetry anthology
reads like the america I know?

or sounds like the chrome tipped
cherry-bombed idle of a lowered *bomba* at the stoplight
with a tattered page manuscript
lying under a pile of sorry assed
thank you for your interest
rejection letters carpeting the floor? ■

Lisa Gill
Dry Spell Dream

In England I fell into a stream pretending
to be a horse, leaping. Last night, I walked
the banks of a river, looking for a place
to cross. It was so thoughtful, this foresight
of my subconscious. Usually I just dive in
but then, often it's a lagoon, or an ocean, or
a giant bowl of chicken soup. Not long ago
I was swimming in an opaque with Johnny
Cash. So placid. Our heads gliding across
the surface, hands just breaking the water
to breast stroke. We must have had fins
on our feet, so sleek and silent. Here though,
was a river with shifting currents and rapids.
I headed upstream looking for a lull in white
water, looking for a trickle, something wade-
able, looking for a bridge. The water kept
rising, the bank narrowing. I held the hand
of a small girl as we approached the source.

Jasmine Sena Cuffee

Women in Slam

An Albuquerque poet, Jasmine Sena Cuffee was City Champion in 2006 and a member of the 2004 Albuquerque Slam Team.

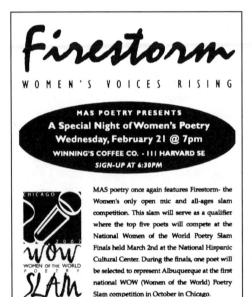

Figure 24. Flyer for Firestorm,
a Quarterly Slam for Women.
Courtesy of Maresa Thompson

Winning the Slam championship was a great accomplishment, especially being that the last four or five years it's been a male ball game. I love my brothers, but it was about damn time that the women got a little attention. In the past two years there's been an influx of strong, passionate, powerful women, ranging in ages and races. They come clear from out the blue and tear shit up. There's never been a large group of women slammers here, which has aided the male dominance, but we're growing in awesome numbers and winning. This, by far, has been the biggest inspiration for me. Don't let anyone tell you I won just because I'm woman. Nobody threw me one. I performed my ass off that night and steadily climbed to first place, gladly taking the crown from my beautiful husband Aaron Cuffee. It's been a hell of a trip, and there are no signs of stopping yet. ■

Jasmine Sena Cuffee
I Dare You

I ask you
Scar me with art
Lick my wounds with words and hum
Songs that have yet to be sung

Outline your poetics on my back
To retrace lost tracks of memories

Become immortal

And tattoo yourself to my soul
Where you will later roll off my tongue
Into deep lakes of me

I once offered you a full cup
And dared you to drink
Oceans have never left you so thirsty ■

Maresa Irene Thompson

Women and Poetry

There is a void in the poetry community. A disparity exists at many readings that are often male-dominated, yet the audience is filled with women poets who aren't sharing.

Many women feel their poetry is intensely personal—a deep projection of themselves. We internalize any negative responses by audience or judges as a rejection of our very essence. Some also feel that their work is simply not good enough to share or are intimidated by performing. As women we can be the harshest judges of ourselves.

Women innately support, encourage, and nourish others. There were a large number of women producing the 2005 National Poetry Slam, yet the one woman on Albuquerque's team was too young to perform onstage during the event. It's time we start to nurture ourselves, foster our own potential, and overcome our fears and inhibitions.

Firestorm, a women-only poetry reading, is about women's voices rising. The Firestorm series was resurrected by the men of Albuquerque's poetry community who saw the void. This event inspires participation because the poets know they will be heard and understood in a welcoming and non-threatening environment. My deepest hope is that Firestorm encourages more women poets to share at other events.

The world needs women's voices. They remind us of who we are and where we came from. They speak of what it is to be a warrior, a mother, a wise woman and look to who we are becoming.

Maresa Irene Thompson
Freshwater Fish

Don't give me your
reincarnated Charlie Parker
story again.

I've about as much stomach
for that as I have for
month old bread.

It's not that I don't like
the story the way I listen to
the same song over and over
until I'm swimming
through it.

It's that I've heard that story
for half a century
over and over
I've been swimming in
Kerouac's Charlie Parker
for miles and your
reincarnated Charlie Parker
whose fingers are magic
is only a projection of the wishes
you have for your pen and lips
to bop out poetry and to be
the Kerouac for this age.

I wonder what words
Lady Day and Ella would sing
of their own
not Cole Porter's.

You're swimming in spaghetti strings
of the same adjectives and adverbs
preoccupying your paper.

I wanted to tell you the story of
what water means to desert people.
I only end up drowning in a
saltwater chorus of the same voices.

But
thunderheads
are beginning
to form. ■

Dale Harris

Poets and Writers Picnic

Local poet Dale Harris has been organizing public poetry perfor-mances for years. Her readings have provided a constant venue for reading poetry without judges, without Slam. Even so, Dale is at slams more often than not. Her support of the Slam community has kept the emphasis on what matters—poetry—reminding both page and performance poets that the goals of each are the same.

The Poets and Writers Picnic is a popular annual summer event held in Mountainair, New Mexico, a ranching and rail-roading town in rural central New Mexico, fifty miles south-east of Albuquerque. It takes place outdoors at the historic Shaffer Hotel on the last Saturday in August during the town's Sunflower Festival, a small town frolic that includes tradi-tional folk art and craft sales, a fancy sunflower hat contest, a chile cook-off, and demonstrations in blacksmithing and sheep dog herding. Sponsored by the Manzano Mountain Arts Council, the Poets and Writers Picnic is my heart child and has continued uninterrupted since 1997. During a several year period when the Shaffer Hotel closed pending new own-ership, artists Dorothy Baker and John Davidson graciously offered their grounds at Tohu Bohu Gallery, better known as the Old Schoolhouse. The Shaffer Hotel completed a major renovation in 2005.

In this high desert region, shade trees and grassy lawns are rare. The lush green of the hotel's gazebo park invites audience members to go barefoot, spread picnic lunches on blankets, and settle in for a highly entertaining afternoon of original poetry and fiction. Authors read from their own works interspersed with a lively open mic and music from local performers. Features at early Poets and Writers Picnics included legendary poet Jimmy Santiago Baca, mystery writer Michael McGarrity, novelists Sharon Niederman and Stephen Ausherman, poets Judyth Hill, María Leyba, E. A. "Tony" Mares, Todd Moore, and Slam pioneers Danny Solis and Don McIver. In 2005 I added a Sunflower Poetry Writing Workshop at the Shaffer Hotel, with Greg Candela as cofacilitator. Participants stay overnight at the Shaffer, write poems together, then share them at an old-fashioned campfire and next day attend the Poets and Writers Picnic. ■

Carol Lewis

the rag *and Herland*

Poet and editor of the rag.

Shortly after my husband John and I settled in Albuquerque in January 2001, I began searching for a connection to the poetry community. A notice in a giveaway paper mentioned a women's poetry group named Herland meeting at the Harwood Art Center. Puzzled by this division of the sexes that I'd never encountered in California workshops, I gave it a try and met a marvelously talented group of individuals under the leadership of superbly gifted poet Sarah McKinstry-Brown.

the rag grew out of these readings originated by Lisa Gill, herself a gifted poet, who organized and edited *the rag* from November 1997 to December 1999, when other activities interfered and she turned her responsibilities over to Sarah. In July 2000, Sarah resigned and moved to Nebraska to begin a marriage and a family, and with her husband continues with readings throughout the Midwest.

Lou Liberty became the next director/editor from August 2001 to April 2002 until she, too, found the responsibilities too time consuming. The mission statement for that period read "to build a foundation of trust and communication and support between women, so that in the long run, women's voices become a more integral part of the larger literary community and in turn—the world."

Darcel Sandland, a member of the group, volunteered to assume editorship of *the rag*, although she was in the process of moving to Colorado. We set up an arrangement. She mailed the pasted-up dummy copies to me, and I'd trot over to our local UPS store and Xerox and distribute them.

Several members volunteered to help by distributing copies in their areas.

In the winter of 2003, Darcel decided the work was interfering with her job as an art teacher and other interests and resigned. We skipped a few issues until I accepted the post. My first effort was the March 2003 issue. Although the distribution system continued, I felt the need to expand and attract new voices, so in June 2003 we went co-ed. Any fear the women may have felt of being overwhelmed was groundless. The proportion of poems we publish generally run 60–40 in their favor.

The result is the familiar broadsheet format you see today in our wall-hung or counter boxes. We retained the name, since the term "rag" is slang for a newspaper or journal (when the paper had a rag content).

We value poems that are original, creative, thoughtful, and expressive—any style, any subject.

We are now in our fifth year under my editorship, and I have derived great joy from reading and printing new poems and new poets writing poems of such high quality.

the rag has been and continues to be free (except for subscriptions to out-of-town readers), since we believe that poetry should have the widest possible dissemination. ▪

Carol Lewis
War

Whoever wins and combs the battlefield
for weapons, whoever loses and flees
in disarray . . . are mirror images

Black in Minares's painting thickens
to a leathery texture, seeps over the frame,
an oil sludge drips on wheat fields, buries
home and cities, swallows the countryside.

Your grandfather's pocket watch, your mother's
rings surrender, likewise your arteries, arm
and leg bones, blackened, crushed edge to edge

If the painting were mine, I'd slash
it from the frame, string it on wire,
plant it in the center of my garden
coax orioles and goldfinch to ruffle fiery
sun feathers, perch on the painting's
sturdy shoulders, wound it with their droppings
(which fertilize the soil) let iridescent
spiders spin webs across the hole in the
upper left quadrant where the heart should be ▪

Daniel S. Solis

Aftermath: The Wider Community

Albuquerque Slam poets have been going into local schools almost since the inception of the Poetry Slam in Albuquerque in 1995. With virtually no budget, no training, and only a vague plan as to what they would actually do once they got there, 'Burque Slam poets began bravely venturing into high schools to, "I don't know, kick some poems . . ."

These early appearances would often be nothing more than local Slam poets getting onstage in an assembly or classroom setting and performing original poems, one after another, in round robin style, and hopefully editing out offensive language on the fly.

Over the years 'Burque Slam poets have become increasingly professional and effective in their approach to getting students interested in poetry. While the performance element of poets in the schools remains a vibrant and necessary constant, extensive and detailed instruction in all things poetic, from generating free verse to formalism to performance techniques, has become the norm.

As 'Burque Slam poets have become ubiquitous features in the classroom so have the funding sources for these vital activities increased. The Harwood Art Center, the National Hispanic Cultural Center (NHCC), and the City of Albuquerque's Cultural Services Department have all given generous financial support to the educational endeavors of 'Burque's Poetry Slam community. The result of these concerted efforts has been a plethora of youth-oriented poetry activities in Albuquerque and the surrounding state—from high school slam teams attending national competitions to audience participation poetry shows for elementary students to the highly respected Voces summer creative writing program at the NHCC to the inception of a statewide middle school poetry slam that in 2006 had eight teams participating and by 2007 had grown to twenty-four teams. Many high schools have hired poets to teach students in slam clubs after school, including Albuquerque High School, Eldorado High School, Robert F. Kennedy Charter High School, and the South Valley Academy.

Albuquerque Slam poets have performed, mentored, and taught at high, middle, and elementary schools, universities, community centers, detention centers, libraries, and art centers in and around Albuquerque. The Albuquerque Slam Team got invited to perform at a National Democratic fundraiser in 2006 and at the City of Albuquerque's Fourth of July celebration as part of its Tricentennial. Women poets are invited to the Association for Women in Communications meetings. Libraries host Slam poets during Poetry Month. Partly a result of the tireless work of Slam poets to infiltrate the community, establish the legitimacy and vibrancy of spoken word, and prove its ability to capture the attention and power of young voices, Sandia Prep and Albuquerque Academy now incorporate poetry in their summer programs. 516 Arts has created an ongoing poetry series, 516 words. Donkey Gallery invited Lisa Gill to curate a book of poetry and writings called the *Donkey Journal.* I hosted events at the National Hispanic Cultural Center's annual music festival, Globalquerque, and the Carnuel Parade and Fiesta at the Harwood Art Center with the Sawmill and Wells Park communities.

Poetry, and spoken word in particular, has moved to the forefront of people's consciousness, and more organizations and institutions recognize that including it enriches their programming. Slam poets' presence as educators, performers, and mentors only continues to grow. ■

Figure 25. Middle School Slam Flyer: VE=NT 2007. *Courtesy of Kenn Rodriguez*

Daniel S. Solis
Song for Solomon

I take my godson Solomon from his mother's arms.
He is six months old, frisky, feisty, ready to play.
Within a minute he tears out one of my earrings,
tries to eat it, then when I stop him,
happily karate chops me in the face.
We sit, read *Hop on Pop*, talk for a while.
He pulls my locks, yanks my beard, and twists my nose.
He is having a busy day.
We are comfortable in the easy chair.
He starts to drift, and I watch the news with the sound turned down,
sanitized images of the war.
It could be ESPN with ammo and weapons,
no thump of mortar or
clamor of machine gun,
no heat of desert
or keen of weeping.

Little Solomon makes soft suckling sounds his sleep,
and slowly it surfaces in my soul—
if the world in its terrible dark appetite wants him,
I cannot stop it—
and I more afraid of this thought than I have ever been of anything before.

I think of the Palestinian man and boy
who left their house one day to buy a used car,
father and son on a happy errand that turned into a fire fight.
A bullet found the boy,
and the day ran red
into the hungry desert streets.
In a taxi the father tried to get him to a hospital,
but the soldiers at the checkpoint saw the boy and said no.
They would not let them through.

The hospital less than a mile beyond the barricade
the soldiers smoking, talking, laughing,
the father begged,
was ignored,
he threatened,
was watched,
he wept,
alone.

Did he sing to his son, as he died that day?
Did the sounds
catch in his throat
as hope became a song with no words
and a melody he couldn't remember?

And I think,
what if that man were me,
and that boy my Solomon?

What dark unexpected garden in the heart then?
What terrible flowers then?
Nightmare panoply of blossoms
each opening its baleful mouth full of jagged teeth
to whisper
then moan
then chant
one word—
revenge . . .

. . . and I know
if that child were the baby boy in my arms now
I know,
I would not be strong enough,
not good enough
to turn away from that evil.

I know,
I would take the vow and make my will
and say,
"Bring me the vest of plastic explosives, more than one.
This hollow body is strong. Load me and dress me and
send me to the checkpoint or the crowded market or the wedding.
I have a gift of blood and fire and wailing
to bestow upon you for taking what I loved most."

But I push away these dark imaginings. . . .
I click off the TV and stare into the half light.
Little Solomon is restless now
and so I try to sing to him.

(Lullaby sung to the tune of "Kiane," by Olu Dara)
Oh Solomon,
won't you go,
go to sleep my baby boy?
Oh Solomon,
won't you close your eyes?
My little baby boy,
I told you some stories,
then you karate chopped me in the face and tore my earrings out tonight,
but you just don't want to go to sleep.
It's alright . . .

I hold him tighter—
he breathes softly—
we are in the world.

Mikaela Renz

Aftermath: Organizing Community

Don't laugh, but I actually have a degree in community planning. Yes, there is such a thing. In my day job, I help build communities at the neighborhood level in Albuquerque. In my summer job, I try to do the same thing among teen writers at the National Hispanic Cultural Center as one of the mentors of the Voces program run by Education Director Shelle Luaces.

This is all to say that I understand what it takes to build community, and I believe it's one of the most important activities any of us can take on in our lives. For those without money or political power, community is sometimes the best source of strength, and solace.

At times, I've found myself trying to explain why I feel so motivated to give back-bending amounts of time to helping organize poetry events that I'm not actually part of. My answer: *because poets have a sense of community like the best communities have.*

It may surprise many people to hear that poets are organized, or at least Slam poets, anyway. It's true! They're hardly ever on time, broke almost always, but they know how to network, share resources, and leverage support. Like most folks with limited resources, they have to in order to survive and thrive. Isn't that what community building is all about? Poets compete and fight amongst themselves like any good family, but when it's all said and done, they love the same things and give their lives to this strange pursuit for a reason.

These poets have built Slam families in each of their cities as well as nationally—and even internationally. They've done this for themselves, for their art, and for their larger communities. Time and again, you hear poets say that writing has saved their lives. When they take the next brave leap and perform onstage, their faith in the power of connection to an audience can sometimes save others.

Because of the unique nature of what they do—communicating through poetry—the community they build is one that celebrates culture, diversity, humor, intelligence, silliness, harnessed political rage, but above all, communication itself. These poets master the power of the word to bring us together to listen to each other and celebrate what we have in common, learn what we don't, hear what we need to, and grow together.

You may think this just sounds good, but I've experienced the tangible results of all this organizing work. In 2006, I found myself completely comfortable—in fact entitled—to stay for a week at a complete stranger's house in Boston (here's my shout-out thanks to Eric Darby—and Adam Rubinstein, who brokered the connection, despite the fact that he barely knew Eric himself!). No, I'd never met my host. Yes, it was fine. Why? Because we're poets. That's what poets do. We travel. We're broke. We stay with poets. We open our doors to traveling poets in return. That's the code.

Nationals is that instinct times ten. Everywhere you go, poets are giving each other ecstatic embraces of reunion—poets of every color, shape, size, background, and sexual preference from everywhere in the country. Despite the omnipresent electric crackle of competition, there is also the enveloping sense of acceptance and support and yes, *community*.

You can see that same circus on a smaller scale at any poetry slam in any city that's worked for years to build its scene. Think of it. How many venues in how many cities across the nation host these events centered on *poetry* and supported and organized and nurtured by *poets*? Hundreds.

It's this generosity and optimism that make it irresistible—and rewarding—to help out. I'm not a performance poet, yet I'm accepted into this crazy community because I do what I can and value what they do and what they give to all of us. I'm honored to be among those who support these poets, to be in the same company as the other folks in this book, the unsung heroes who support art in all its guises because they understand its importance to our communities.

One of the best examples is the Harwood Art Center, mothership of spoken word in Albuquerque. Along with all the other amazing artistic activities it spearheads and supports, Harwood outdid itself with the 2006 *Harwood Anthology*, which was envisioned and executed by the inimitable Susan McAllister, and featured both celebrated and underground poets in and around Albuquerque.

This book is that anthology Nationals-sized. It's a small token of appreciation for years of Albuquerque Slam effort. These poets have earned every second of the recognition they receive. We owe them our thanks. The best part is knowing that all the praise they get goes into opening doors and increasing opportunities for other poets around them; that's just the Slam code. If only all our communities and organizing efforts could follow this model. ▧

Mikaela Renz
Monsoon Season
August 1, 2006, Albuquerque, New Mexico, USA

We watch hate billow upward in the east
the way we analyze a coming storm,

reflexively pick up an umbrella
to shield ourselves from the worst wet,

ponder a sunnier day,
plan a night in
snuggled
by our TV,

curse the momentary inconvenience
of water waves in flooded streets,

the ineptitude of other drivers
who grew up here, too,

but seem to know less than we do
about how to drive in rain,

blithely ignore
building evidence of climate change

the way I fool myself into thinking
my meanness to you

on certain days
is a passing phase

having nothing to do
with punishing you

for those little things
I imagine you've done to me

because I didn't hear you say
you're hurting, too,

distracted,
slammed with life,

caught under the weight
of everyone's expectations

piled
on your own.

Perhaps it is unfair
to expect sunshine

in Israel
when I can't count on myself

to be nice
to the man I love

on a hard day
that didn't end in bloodshed.

Maybe I should fear
the increasing intensity of storms

in a desert state
whether or not my neighbors learn better how to drive.

Correlation
is causation

in a universe
where all is relative

and time
flows both ways.

Chaos creates order
when the tsunami crashes the butterfly's wings.

Responsibility reverses
time's tide.

It is the only thing
that can hold back the wave.

We can choose
not to let blood

the way I can bite my cutting tongue
in order to ask you

about your day
and listen to the rain

stop grief for a moment
at home.

In this way
I can expect the butterfly

to shuttle diplomacy
all the way

to the middle
east. ■

Marc Smith
Pull the Next One Up

When you get to the top of the mountain
Pull the next one up.
Then there'll be two of you
Roped together at the waist
Tired and proud, knowing the mountain,
Knowing the human force it took
To bring both of you there.
And when the second one has finished
Taking in the view,
Satisfied by the heat and perspiration under the wool,
Let her pull the next one up;
Man or woman, climber of mountains.
Pull the next hand over
The last jagged rock
To become three.
Two showing what they've already seen.
And one knowing now the well-being with being
Finished with one mountain,
With being able to look out a long way
Toward other mountains.
Feeling a temptation to claim victory
As if mountains were human toys to own.
When you ask how high is this mountain
With a compulsion to know
Where you stand in relationship to other peaks,
Look down to wherefrom you came up
And see the rope that's tied to your waist
Tied to the next man's waist,
Tied to the next woman's waist,
Tied to the first man's waist,
To first woman's waist . . . and pull the rope!

Never mind the flags you see flapping on conquered pinnacles.
Don't waste time scratching inscriptions into the monolith.
You are the stone itself.
And each man, each woman up the mountain,
Each breath exhaled at the peak,
Each glad-I-made-it . . . here's-my-hand,
Each heartbeat wrapped around the hot skin of the sun-bright sky,
Each noise panted or cracked with laughter,
Each embrace, each cloud that holds everyone
in momentary doubt . . .
All these are inscriptions of a human force that can
Conquer conquering hand over hand pulling the rope
Next man up, next woman up.
Sharing a place, sharing a vision.
Room enough for all on all the mountain peaks.
Force enough for all
To hold all the hanging bodies
Dangling in the deep recesses of the mountain's belly
Steady . . . until they have the courage . . .
Until they know the courage . . .
Until they understand
That the only courage there is:
To pull the next man up
Pull the next woman up
Pull the next up

Up

Up. ◾

V. B. PRICE
Afterword

Poet, teacher, scholar, columnist, mentor, critic, and thinker, V. B. Price has championed and channeled the unique personality of Albuquerque, adding his voice to its creative, cultural, and social chorus.

Slam poetry competitions have brought poetry back full circle to its performance origins, when poetry not only created mythology and commented on the human condition, but was also a major form of collective entertainment. Performance poetry in ancient Greece, by rhapsodes reciting Homer, spawned Greek theater, a hybrid of epic and lyric poetry, that evolved into a cultural mirror of collective soul-searching and psychological relief in Greek city-states. When Albuquerque's Poetry Slam Team won the National Slam Championship in 2005, it was, along with the other Slam performers, continuing an ancient tradition of creative competition best known in the theatrical contests during the Greater Dionysia in Athens.

Performance poetry has widened the audience for American poetry in a way that would never have been dreamed of even thirty years ago. The audiences at the Albuquerque Slam competition reminded me of what happens in countries that love their poets. Russian poets, for instance, can draw immense crowds and become national heroes because they are willing to say what no one else will and take risks that no one else dares.

The miseries often suffered at traditional poetry readings, even by those who love poetry, have become almost cliché. Poets, it's asserted, are terrible readers of their own work. They don't know how to perform. They "drone on," turning something that could be exciting into a kind of suffering embarrassment causing eyelids to crash shut. Of course, clichés are half-truths. There are many poets who read their poems brilliantly and with gusto: Dylan Thomas, Ezra Pound, Robert Duncan, W. H. Auden, Allen Ginsberg, Gary Snyder, and New Mexico's Winfield Townley Scott, Jimmy Santiago Baca, Joan Logghe, Miriam Sagan, Robert Lloyd, Larry Goodell, David Johnson, Simon Ortiz, Demetria Martínez, and Levi Romero. As performers of modern poetry, despite their own cultural traditions, their presence as powerful readers has associations with not only Homer and brilliant lyric performers like Sappho, but also with Celtic bards, Scandinavian and Icelandic skalds, Anglo-Saxon scops, and a galaxy of unnamed storytellers and epic singers in every town and tribe. Oral epic poetry in pre-Roman Europe, for instance, gave us poets who not only composed their poems on the spot, in their heads, often in the heat of battle, but then had to perform them from memory before a hall of warriors fresh from the kill. If they droned on, chances are they would lose their place at the table, if not their heads.

My hope is that Slam poetry—with its competitive enthusiasm and sense of community—will continue to have an expanding influence, not to turn everyone into slammers—slamming takes a special gift—but to make it clear that traditional poetry has a vibrant potential audience again, one that is waiting for all poets to read out loud as if their culture depended on them. ▪

A BIGGER BOAT: CD

Selected Poems and Radio Spots

Produced by Don McIver

1. **KUNM Spot**
0:33

2. **Rebel Music**
Hakim Bellamy and
Carlos Contreras
2:55

3. **Pink and Brown**
Aaron Cuffee
3:14

4. **Stereotype**
Hakim Bellamy, Carlos Contreras,
Kenn Rodriguez, and Aaron Cuffee
3:05

5. **We Teach**
Hakim Bellamy, Carlos Contreras,
Kenn Rodriguez, and Aaron Cuffee
2:45

6. **KISS-KIOT Radio Spot**
1:03

7. **Billie's Blues**
Jessica Lopez
3:05

8. **Gunslinger**
Hakim Bellamy and
Lee Francis IV
2:55

9. **Song for Solomon**
Daniel S. Solis
3:41

10. **Dos Gordos Guapos**
Damien Flores and
Lee Francis IV
3:28

11. **I Am**
Kenn Rodriguez
3:16

12. **KBAC-KSFQ Radio Spot**
0:31

13. **Prayer Piece**
Hakim Bellamy and
Carlos Contreras
1:56

14. **Novena Pa La Tierra**
Damien Flores
1:34

15. **God's Army**
Don McIver
2:39

16. **Art is Life**
Carlos Contreras
3:19

17. **KTEG Radio Spot**
0:34

18. **Loss**
Hakim Bellamy and
Damien Flores
3:14

19. **Minutemen**
Jessica Lopez and
Damien Flores
2:44

20. **Many Voices**
Hakim Bellamy, Carlos Contreras,
Aaron Cuffee, and Damien Flores
2:46

21. **A Question of Civil Rights**
Hakim Bellamy
3:43

22. **KOB Radio Spot**
1:01